SERIES TEACHING FILM AND M

Teaching TV Soaps

Lou Alexander and Alison Cousens

with additional material by Eileen Lewis

Series Editor: Vivienne Clark
Commissioning Editor: Wendy Earle

British Library Cataloguing-in-Publication Data
A catalogue record for this book is available from the British Library

ISBN 0 85170 978 8

First published in 2004 by the British Film Institute
21 Stephen Street, London W1T 1LN

Copyright © British Film Institute 2004
The copyright of this teaching guide belongs to the British Film Institute.

Student worksheets to support this guide are supplied at: www.bfi.org.uk/tfms
User name: **tvsoap** Password: **te1101so**

It is a breach of copyright to copy this guide or the worksheets, except for educational purposes. If you would like to reproduce anything in this pack for any other purpose, please contact the Resources Editor, *bfi* Education, 21 Stephen Street, London W1T 1LN.

Design: Amanda Hawkes
Cover photograph: *EastEnders* courtesy of *bfi* Stills
Printed in Great Britain by: Cromwell Press Ltd

www.bfi.org.uk

The British Film Institute offers you opportunities to experience, enjoy and discover more about the world of film and television.

Contents

Introduction to the series   1

1 Introduction   2
Assessment contexts   4
Why teach TV soaps?   6
Approaches to teaching   6
How to use this guide   9
Schemes of work   9

2 Key concepts   14
Institutions   14
Forms and conventions   24
Audiences   36
Representations and ideology   42

3 Case studies   48
Case study 1: *EastEnders* : 'Bloody, bleak and brilliant'   48
Case study 2: *Neighbours* : Everybody needs them?   58
Case study 3: *Coronation Street*: Paradise on Earth   64
Case study 4: *Hollyoaks*: Low fat soap   76

Glossary   85
Bibliography and further reading   89

Introduction to the series

The recent, rapid growth of both Film and Media Studies post-16 has inevitably led to a pressing demand for more teachers for these popular courses. But, given the comparatively recent appearance of both subjects at degree level (and limited availability of specialist post-graduate teaching courses), both new and experienced teachers from other disciplines are faced with teaching either subject for the first time, without a degree-level background to help them with subject content and conceptual understanding.

In addition, the recent post-16 specifications (syllabi) saw the arrival of new set topics and areas of study, and some of the specifications have frequently changing topics, so there is a pressing need for up-to-date resources to help teacher preparation.

This series has been developed specifically with these factors – and the busy teacher – in mind. Each title aims to provide teachers with an accessible reference resource, with essential topic content, as well as clear guidance on good classroom practice to improve the quality of their teaching and their students' learning. Every author in the series is an experienced practitioner of Film and/or Media Studies at this level and many have examining/moderating experience. It has been a pleasure to work closely with such a diverse range of professionals and I should like to thank them for their individual contributions to the series.

Key features
- Assessment contexts
- Suggested schemes of work
- Historical contexts (where appropriate)
- Key facts, statistics and terms
- Detailed reference to the key concepts of Film and Media Studies
- Detailed case studies
- Glossaries
- Bibliographies
- Student worksheets, activities and resources (available online) – ready for you to print and photocopy for the classroom.

Current and forthcoming titles in the series include:
Teaching Scriptwriting, Screenplays and Storyboards for Film and TV Production; Teaching TV Sitcom; Teaching Digital Video Production; Teaching TV News; Teaching Women and Film; Teaching World Cinema; Teaching British Broadcasting since 1990; Teaching Analysis of Film Language and Production; Teaching British Cinema since 1990; Teaching Video Games; Teaching Film Censorship and Controversy; Teaching Analysis of TV Language and Production; Teaching Music Videos.

SERIES EDITOR: Vivienne Clark is a former Head of Film and Media Studies. She is an Advanced Skills Teacher, an Associate Tutor of the British Film Institute and Principal Examiner for A Level Media Studies for one of the English awarding bodies. She is a freelance teacher trainer and writer/editor on Film and Media Studies, with several published textbooks, including *GCSE Media Studies* (Longman 2002) and *Key Concepts & Skills for Media Studies* (Arnold 2002). She is also a course tutor on the BFI/Middlesex University MA Level module: An Introduction to Media Education (distance learning).

Authors:
Lou Alexander has taught Film and Media since 1990 and is currently working at Brighton, Hove and Sussex Sixth Form College. She also worked for the WJEC awarding body in the capacity of Coursework Moderator for several years and last year acted as an assistant examiner for the FS3 paper for A Level Film Studies. During the last two years she has worked in a mainly freelance capacity writing and designing for the BFI, and teaching filming and editing skills to children in the East End of London.
Alison Cousens is Head of Media, Film and Communication Studies at Brighton Hove and Sussex Sixth Form College. She has been teaching Media Studies at GCSE, AS and A Level since 1992 and is currently teaching undergraduates part time, while completing an MA in Digital Media at Sussex University.
Eileen Lewis teaches Media Studies and English at Maidstone Grammar School in Kent. She is Chief Examiner for GCSE Media Studies for one of the English awarding bodies, an experienced A Level Media Studies examiner, a freelance teacher trainer and writer of several textbooks, including *GCSE Media Studies* (Longman 2002), *Key Concepts and Skills for Media Studies* (Arnold 2002) and *Teaching TV News* (2003) for this series.

Introduction

'Precinct pulp' (The Guardian, 3 November, 2003) or 'the template against which we measure reality'? (Mark Lawson, *The Soap Opera: Fiction or Reality*, BBC2, 1999).

Despite its populist image, the soap opera has been the focus of much academic study over the years, and for good reason. Since the form first appeared on American radio in the 1930s, it has drawn worldwide audiences in millions. Today in the UK, television's most watched soaps regularly attract upwards of ten million viewers per episode, quite a feat in today's highly competitive multichannel environment.

Their stars are household names, whose celebrity lifestyles and antics fill the pages of tabloid newspapers. The programmes' storylines also provide essential content for many magazines and newspapers, either in the form of reviews and comment or scoops and spoilers of forthcoming episodes (with which the soaps' producers are usually complicit). The contemporary setting allows for the discussion of issues that are relevant or important to viewers. Furthermore, audience loyalty is strong and long-lived, as is apparent in the many fan websites. In addition, there is often a clear link between programmes and government health and education policy, whereby the producers often develop storylines that match current popular and ministerial interest, in topics related to crime, old age or health.

Consequently, the genre has become a staple area of study for the media student. Its generic characteristics are highly recognisable and its popularity ensures that student knowledge is detailed and enthusiastically revealed. The genre also provides a good springboard for the further study of relevant media theory, such as those associated with audience consumption, effects and spectatorship, and realism. Soaps also offer excellent opportunities for the investigation of ideological messages and values.

This pack is aimed at teachers whose familiarity with these issues, on an academic level, may be limited. It references the key Media Studies concepts and provides background information on the various theoretical frameworks. Each of the study areas set out in the media specifications (below), forms and conventions, audiences, institutions, and representation, is covered to help teachers plan the course. This guide includes four sample schemes of work, while online worksheets provide suggestions for classroom activities, including a practical synoptic project that tests a range of skills.

Note: See *Teaching British Broadcasting since 1990* by Rachel Viney (2004), also in this series, for detailed explanations of the institutional contexts of British television and essential background information to help you teach the TV soaps topic to students. A forthcoming title in this series, *Teaching Analysis of Television Language and Production*, should also be useful.

Assessment contexts

	Awarding Body & Level	Subject	Unit Code	Module/Topic
✓	OCR A2 Level	Media Studies	2735	Media Issues and Debates Topic: British Television Soap Opera
✓	AQA AS/A2 Level	Media Studies	A2 Mod. 4 A2 Mod. 6	Text and Contexts in the Media Comparative Critical Analysis
✓	WJEC AS/A2 Level	Media Studies	Unit 1 Unit 2 Unit 4	Modern Media Forms Media Representations and Reception Investigating Media Texts
✓	AQA A2 Level	Communication Studies	Module 5	Culture, Context and Communication
✓	EdExcel AVCE	Media Studies	Unit 1	Communication and Production Analyse Media Products
✓	SQA Higher	Media Studies	D6V1 D6V3 D6TV	Broadcast Narratives Television Representations

OCR Media Studies A2

Unit 2735 Media Issues and Debates – British Television Soap Opera
This synoptic unit expects students to be able to comment on all the key study areas: Forms and conventions, institutions, audiences and representations.

AQA Media Studies AS/A2

Module 4 – Texts and Contexts in the Media
Teachers choose two areas from four specified topics. Soap could be included in three of the topics: representations, genre and media audiences.

Module 6 – Comparative Critical Analysis
This synoptic unit requires comparative studies of texts like soap. Suggested examples are:
- The same genre from different historical periods
- The same theme treated by different media
- The same genre with different media audiences.

Students could look at soaps from different eras and analyse how they have reflected changing attitudes through representations of situations and characters. They might investigate how soaps are designed to appeal to specific audiences, perhaps through a comparison of *Coronation Street* and *Hollyoaks*. (See Case studies 3 and 4.)

WJEC Media Studies AS/A2

Unit 1 – Modern Media Forms
Involves the study of key areas of narrative and genre. TV soap, with its identifiable narrative and genre codes, would be a good example.

Unit 2 – Media Representations and Reception
This guide provides specific information on stereotyping, effects models and debates, theories of audience reception and realism, all of which are identified in the specification.

Unit 4 – Investigating Media Texts
A comparative study of two texts which must centre around one or more of the following concepts: genre, representations or narrative form. The case studies would prove particularly useful.

AQA Communication Studies A2

Module 5 – Culture, Context and Communication
This theory-based unit focuses on culture, ideology, identity and modes of address. Concepts of high and popular culture and ideology are easily investigated through a study of TV soap.

EdExcel AVCE Media Studies: Communication and Production

Unit 1 – Analyse Media Products
Focuses on representations, genre and narrative structure; TV soap, with its highly identifiable narrative and genre codes, would be a good example.

Why teach TV soaps?

Teaching soap opera can be surprisingly challenging, considering that students are often very familiar with the genre. However, its very familiarity means students are not used to approaching it in an intellectual or academic way. It is important to both draw on students' knowledge and extend it into new, more rigorous intellectual territory. Below is some advice on how to manage this with the wide range of abilities and levels of expertise you are likely to meet in the classroom. More specific teaching suggestions are included in the introduction to the online worksheets and in the case studies.

Approaches to teaching

- Soap opera often generates extreme views
  Students tend to feel quite strongly about soap opera, both positively and negatively. This is often (though not always) split along gender lines. It is worthwhile using this strength of feeling at the start:

  - To get a sense of students' tastes, preferences and prejudices;
  - To generate discussion and debate (which will develop as their grasp of theory improves);
  - To encourage students to appreciate alternative points of view and to learn how to defend their own in an informed manner.

  A good way to channel and focus these extreme opinions is class discussion. Separate students into 'fans' and 'sceptics'. Divide the class (or get students to work in pairs – one 'fan' and one 'sceptic') and ask each side to present their case to the opposing camp, justifying each point with examples. This is good practice in the construction of an argument and could form a basis from which you can begin to challenge the vaguely formed opinions of 'fans' or the cultural prejudice of 'sceptics'. Through facilitation of this kind of debate, students with strong opinions can be guided towards understanding the validity of alternative points of view and shown the value of supporting their ideas with concrete examples and evidence.

- **Teaching tips**

  - Use students' expertise in the topic
    Individual students may be fans and know particular soaps in great detail. They can be useful in informing the rest of the class, as well as becoming an audience 'case study' themselves (for example, in exploring fan behaviour).

- Don't presume all students know about soap opera
  TV soap is a good topic to teach because most students are familiar with the genre. However, levels of knowledge will vary widely. Some students rarely, if ever, watch soap opera; others have intimate knowledge of current programmes. Both types can be used to investigate audience behaviour and responses. For example, what factors link those students who rarely watch soaps? Why have they resisted the genre? What (if anything) might encourage them to watch soaps? How do these students compare demographically with students who regularly watch soaps? Ask students to brainstorm as many soap characters as they can. It is often surprising how many they know, including from soaps they don't usually watch, or from the past, who they have never actually seen. This can lead to an interesting discussion about the prominence of soap opera in popular culture (radio, magazines, tabloids) and the role of archive knowledge and history in the soap opera genre.

- Get students to do their own audience research
  Encourage students to conduct their own interviews and research. Students who find this kind of work daunting could work collaboratively in a small group. If students have access to video cameras, they can film and edit their interviews (often rough edits in-camera will suffice) to present to the class, with analysis of audience responses and summaries of their findings about consumption, viewing habits and demographics. Tasks like this maintain practical skills and motivate students who might otherwise find academic research difficult or dull.

- Balance familiar with unfamiliar in your case studies
  The main danger with students who are fans of particular soaps is that they will adopt an uncritical approach. It is therefore useful to discover class tastes and preferences in order to balance the examples you use, choosing both familiar and unfamiliar ones. One idea is to put students into groups, depending on their familiarity with particular soaps, and ask them to research a soap opera in detail – looking at key characters, narrative structure, scheduling, history etc. Ask them to present regular case study examples or extracts from their soap to the rest of the class to illustrate the key concepts so they become the class experts on the series. In this way students get into a routine of applying the theories they learn to specific case study examples; they thus consolidate their learning and generate a range of concrete examples which they can use when completing formal written work (examination or coursework) on the topic.

- Become new viewers together
  You may be able to find a soap opera that no one in the class watches, and it is an interesting exercise to become new viewers together, either in groups or as a class. You can share your experiences as an audience,

discuss who the target audience is, who in the class becomes most readily absorbed in the series, and who finds it most difficult to become involved. You might also discuss the problems new viewers encounter with soap opera's narrative form. For example, a new viewer must quickly become familiar with a complex network of already established characters, settings and storylines and this can be quite a disorientating experience, which is useful to analyse. This kind of 'collective new viewer' approach is often a good way of challenging the prejudices of the soap opera sceptics, who may be resistant to viewing soaps on their own, but can be encouraged to realise the complexity of the programme's structure, when asked to approach it analytically as an extended class exercise.

This process can also lead into a discussion of the institutional issues surrounding the need to maintain and increase ratings by attracting and keeping new viewers, while avoiding alienation of the established audience. (At any one time there will be soaps trying to attract new viewers through controversial storylines. If your chosen soap is not currently doing so, you can use other examples.)

- Help students to learn the appropriate academic vocabulary
  One of the problems with a topic like TV soap is that students are used to discussing it, at home or with their peers, in a non-academic way. Students need to beware of adopting a similar informal, or colloquial, register when they are discussing it in the context of formal examinations. However, academic vocabulary can be quite daunting to students and they need to be guided in how to use and apply it. So:

  – Introduce theoretical terms gradually, one at a time;
  – Show students extracts and explain them in an informed theoretical way – focusing on one aspect of film and television theory; for example, camera angles, or narrative structure, or representations, or scheduling practices, or ideology;
  – Ask students to find their own case study examples (either individually or in groups) and present these to the class, explaining how they might be used to illustrate a particular theory;
  – Repeat this kind of pair/group presentation constantly. Gradually, using the appropriate vocabulary to analyse extracts and stills becomes the habitual way for students to perceive and talk about soaps. This should then inform their written responses to the topic's final assessments (either examination- or coursework-based).

- Review key concepts towards the end of the topic
  By the end of a topic students should be routinely collecting their own case study examples and extracts. They should have notes on these extracts

and be able to apply particular concepts and theories. A good way of assessing how confident students are is by giving them a summary of the key concepts taken directly from your chosen assessment specification. For each concept or theoretical term, ask them to write one sentence which summarises what they understand the term to mean and to note down at least one case study example which they could use to illustrate it. This is an effective way of reviewing the topic, trouble-shooting any remaining uneasiness with particular concepts or terms and identifying the areas which need revision.

How to use this guide

Each of the following schemes of work suggests how to approach the study of TV soaps through the key concepts, and presumes an allocation of eight hours of contact time, grouped as three to four two-hour blocks over two weeks. A teacher hoping to cover all four might allocate approximately half a term (five to six weeks) to the study of TV soaps altogether.

These outlines may be adapted for the timetable and groups as appropriate.
- Scheme of work 1: Forms and conventions (genre codes, realism, narrative, etc);
- Scheme of work 2: Institutions (funding, ratings, scheduling, production, etc);
- Scheme of work 3: Audiences (profiles, effects theories, etc);
- Scheme of work 4: Representations (stereotyping, class, race, family, gender roles, ideology, etc).

Worksheets and student handouts to support the schemes of work and teaching suggestions in this guide are available at www.bfi.org.uk/tfms. To access the pages, enter username: **tvsoap**, and password: **te1101so**. If you have any problems, email education.resources@bfi.org.uk.

Schemes of work

1. Forms and conventions

Aims: To promote understanding and awareness of:
- The origins of soap;
- The cultural importance of soap today and historically;
- The importance of genre recognition for both audience and producers;
- The narrative conventions of soap;
- The construction of 'realism' in soaps.

Outcomes:
- To produce an advertisement for a soap tie-in magazine;
- To produce a detailed analysis of one TV soap;
- To write an essay comparing the ways in which two soaps construct realism.

Lesson 1 The history of the soap genre
Class discussion – what do the students already know about soap, who watches what, etc
Provide brief handout outlining the history of soap
Compare extracts from current British and international soaps and archive examples, such as vintage *Coronation Street*
Group exercise – Produce a list of possible companies which might sponsor the most popular soaps today
Design a magazine advertisement which ties in the product and the programme
Research the history of soaps in this country via the internet

Lesson 2 The generic conventions of soap
Class discussion on the soap genre
Group exercise – Students brainstorm a) recurring themes and issues and b) what kind of characters frequently appear in soaps
Discuss the limited locations available to the soap producer and analyse whether this is a drawback
Students make a detailed analysis of how a particular soap conforms to the genre, with reference to characters, settings, themes, etc

Lesson 3 The narrative conventions of soap
Show the closing sequences of several soaps. Class discuss and record common elements of narrative structure
Compare with dramas and docusoaps that are similar, but do not fit into the soap genre
In groups, students discuss a range of programmes and whether they fit into the generic and narrative conventions of soap

Lesson 4 Realism
Outline different approaches to constructing realism. Support with handouts
Give out handout on the 'angry young man' movement and social realism
Illustrate with extracts
Relate to British soaps and compare to American soaps such as *Dallas*

Essay: Compare two British soaps, discussing the ways in which they construct the 'real'

2. Institutions and TV soaps

Aims: To promote understanding and awareness of:
- The history of the BBC, ITV, Channel 4 and their remits;
- The ways in which the institutions are funded;
- The importance of advertisers;
- The importance of scheduling;
- The production processes and personnel;
- Links with other media.

Outcomes:
- To produce a proposal for a new TV soap with three scripted sequences;
- To produce a press release marketing the new TV soap.

Lesson 1 The production contexts of soap
Class discussion on differing histories of the channels and how they are funded
Watch extracts of advertisements in breaks of soaps and compare with those from other programmes to reveal how advertising targets audiences
Provide factual information regarding the cost of advertising in the breaks of different soaps and compare these costs

Lesson 2 Scheduling
Students analyse a daily schedule from a newspaper or listings magazine
Compare audiences and present findings to the class
Students identify the main audiences throughout the day for the main scheduling blocks
Students make a proposal for a new soap and how it could be scheduled

Lesson 3 The production of soap
Provide handout of roles and processes in soap production
Taking the proposal for a new soap that was completed last lesson, students write three three-minute sequences using characters and scenarios thought of before, one of which should contain a cliff-hanger
Students now try to interweave the storylines, cutting and pasting the scripts they have written

Lesson 4 Links with other media
Class discussion on importance of other media to soaps
In groups, students analyse a range of magazines with soap gossip and photos
Students prepare a press release to be sent to entertainment magazines promoting the soap they have been working on, explaining why the characters and what happens to them will be of interest to the magazine's readers
Students research soap websites on the internet, comparing unofficial sites with official ones

3. Audiences for TV soaps

Aims: To promote understanding and awareness of:
- Effects theories;
- Theories of the active audience;
- The behaviour of fans;
- How audiences are categorised by advertisers.

Outcomes: To undertake
- a class survey on the consumption and effects of TV soaps;
- an audience survey on the uses and gratifications of TV soaps.

Lesson 1 Media effects theories
Class discuss handout on theories of effects research, including active/passive audience approaches
In groups, students take a range of examples of different TV genres and assess whether they consider themselves passive consumers or if they use them in a variety of ways
Record conclusions as a class

Lesson 2 Media effects theories in relation to soap
Class discuss how soap audiences have been studied in the context of wider effects debates
Class survey – devise a brief questionnaire to discover what uses and gratifications soaps offered the class
Students produce questionnaires for different audiences, such as children and parents

Lesson 3 The active audience
Recap other sources of information on soap and relate to uses and gratifications theory
Using extracts and statistics (from publications like the Broadcast Standards Commission's report, *Soap Box or Soft Soap*), class discuss and record details on the audience for different soaps

Prepare and conduct audience survey to find out whether soap is in fact a genre watched by 'housewives' or if the audience extends further than this
Students record and evaluate findings

4. Representations in TV soaps

Aims: To promote understanding and awareness of:
- Stereotyping;
- Representations of different groups in TV soaps;
- Ideological values and messages in TV soaps;
- Dominant ideologies.

Outcomes: To produce
- an essay analysing the representations of gender in a range of TV soaps;
- an essay on TV soap and ideology.

Lesson 1 Representation and stereotyping
Students list male and female or regional stereotypes in groups and discuss
Class discussion on whether soap characters are stereotypical, using extracts
Groups analyse male/female characters in different soaps and present findings
Taking one soap, students make notes on female roles and how far they conform to stereotypes

Lesson 2 Ideology and TV soaps
Define ideology and assess how representations of certain social groups might help other groups to maintain their positions of power
List dominant ideologies in Western society, such as: 'We should aspire to being rich', and 'Working hard at our jobs is important'. Discuss whether some groups benefit from their perpetuation
Class examines whether soap tends to promote dominant ideologies
Read through information about hegemonic and pluralist models

Lesson 3 Models of media power and the active/passive audience
Detailed discussion of the hegemonic and pluralist models in relation to soaps
Students record and summarise main points
Outline other useful theories and tie into the effects debate
Essay: To what extent does soap contribute to the creation of 'consensus' in our society?

2

Key concepts

Students should not look at TV soaps in isolation, but consider them in their production and institutional contexts, as well as in terms of genre, narrative and language. As with any media text, all of these contexts contribute to their form, style and ideology and to their popularity with audiences. This chapter provides information to help you explore these contexts with students.

Institutions

● Industry in flux

A record figure of 30 million people tuned in to watch *EastEnders* on Christmas Day in 1986 to watch Dirty Den get the better of his wife Angie. Even today, 'specials' (episodes that focus on one specific storyline for a day or a week, often involving a new location and a limited number of characters – while the rest of the cast go on holiday!) can attract close to 20 million viewers.

The fact that soaps have the power to attract such huge audiences, and maintain them, demonstrates the important role they play for television producers. Today, daily audiences of approximately 10 million regularly watch their favourite soap operas. They can supplement their passion by buying TV and soap magazines or celebrity magazines that frequently feature soap stars (such as Heat, OK! and Hello) or by visiting official and unofficial fan websites.

However, despite the ubiquitous presence of soaps in TV schedules and on newsagents' shelves, compared to viewing figures of 10 to 15 years ago, audiences are falling. This is chiefly because, in today's multichannel television environment, the ratings for terrestrial TV are in decline. The television audience is fragmenting, with fewer viewers watching the same programme at the same time. This has significance for the funding of commercial television (the 'reach' of a particular programme is important to advertisers) and for the profile and support of the UK's prime public service broadcaster, the BBC, funded by the licence fee.

Because of this downward trend, advertisers are unwilling to pay as much for slots between programmes. This slump in advertising revenue is evident across the broadcasting and advertising sector, for the reasons given above, and because the internet and mobile phones offer an alternative forum for advertisers. These issues are discussed later in this section (and in greater detail in *Teaching British Broadcasting since 1990*).

But to begin with, students need to understand something of the production contexts:

- Who makes TV soaps?
- Where does the funding come from?
- How are soaps scheduled?
- What processes are involved in making soap operas?
- Why are soap magazines and websites important?

The public service broadcasting (PSB) context

Like every other media product, soaps are dependent upon the production context in which they are constructed. The producers of the BBC soap, *EastEnders*, have to be aware that they are spending public money when they make the programme as the BBC is funded by the licence fee.

As part of the tradition of public service broadcasting, the programme has to be of high quality while reflecting the tastes and interests of a mass audience. Some commentators argue that the BBC's freedom from the need to satisfy advertisers means programme makers should be more adventurous. Others argue that if the style of the programme or the topics covered were to become more experimental, audiences may switch off or change channels. The BBC is increasingly under pressure to maintain as high an audience share as possible for its flagship programmes, in relation to its terrestrial competitors, to justify the licence fee. This factor limits the programme makers to a considerable degree.

The regulation of the BBC through the Royal Charter (due for renewal in 2006) and its Board of Governors also has implications for the amount of political freedom enjoyed by the programme makers (see Representation and ideology, page 42). (The BBC's future management and funding have recently been brought into focus by the Iraq conflict.)

The commercial context

In contrast, *Coronation Street* is made by Granada Television, a commercial company which, with Carlton, owns the largest ITV television franchise. Since 1955, when ITV was set up, the viewing population of Britain has been divided into areas, contracts for which have been franchised to media companies for specific periods of time. In simple terms, these companies make money by selling advertising space or sponsorship spots, to manufacturers and services in the short breaks in and between the programmes. They also receive revenue from investments, other media interests and sales of programmes and back catalogues.

Programmes on commercial channels are funded by this income. As a result, the makers of *Coronation Street* are also under pressure to maintain high audience figures so that advertisers will pay high prices for the advertisement slots. Currently, a 30-second advertising slot within *Coronation Street* can cost at least £50,000. Commercial channels can gain further revenues by offering programmes for sponsorship; *Coronation Street* has been sponsored by Cadbury Ltd for several years. (See Case study 3 on *Coronation Street*.) *Coronation Street*, *Emmerdale*, *Hollyoaks* and *EastEnders* have all had to extend their number of weekly episodes as a result of changing institutional relationships between advertisers, broadcasters and other programming sectors.

Advertising pressures

Since 2000 there has been a slowdown in the world economy that has had a significant effect on advertising revenues. However, fluctuations are an accepted (if disliked and destabilising) part of the economic process, and advertising revenues (to paraphrase the warning on interest rates and shares) go up as well as down. Television companies got a shock in 2001, because advertising revenues, which had been getting steadily higher towards the end of the 1990s, fell suddenly by 11%. However, since then the decline has been less dramatic and they have even risen briefly during special events such as the football World Cup or the Olympics. Although *EastEnders* and *Coronation Street* are funded very differently from each other, both programme makers are subject to the pressure to make their products appealing to a mass audience and thus gain higher ratings.

Channel 4

At its inception, Channel 4's remit was to be innovative and challenging in its approach to programme making. To avoid subjecting the channel to the pressures that come from having to meet the demands of advertisers, it was funded by a levy paid by the ITV companies, who earned this back through selling advertising space on the new channel. This unprecedented move allowed the output of the channel to be quite different from BBC1 and ITV and quickly it became renowned for bringing new forms and previously censored material to British screens. This satisfied the tastes of the relatively young and culturally diverse audience the channel was targeting and, after some initial difficulties, advertisers were happy to buy time on the channel.

However, the 1990 Broadcasting Act removed financial help for the channel and it was forced to become more mainstream in its output in order to be able to sustain itself by its own funding. In 2002 Channel 4's revenue was reduced to such a degree that it was forced to shut down FilmFour (responsible for a significant body of film production projects) and sack over 100 people. The new commercial pressures have also affected Channel 4 soap operas, which have had to compete in the mainstream market.

Brookside (Mersey TV), originated by Phil Redmond, which was launched as the centrepiece of the schedule on the first night of Channel 4 in 1982, was considered quite daring and different to the more established soaps that dominated television. Its characters were younger and their lives apparently more relevant to a youthful audience than those of soaps like *Coronation Street* and *Emmerdale*. However, its ratings slumped to a low of 400,000 in 2002 and it was relegated to a Tuesday night omnibus slot. It finally fell victim to advertising pressures and was axed in November 2003 by Channel 4 Chief Executive Mark Thompson:

> Peak-time schedules have changed radically across British television and are no longer an environment in which Brookside can thrive.

Channel 4 has recently increased the episodes of Mersey TV's *Hollyoaks* (also started by Phil Redmond) from four to five per week, hoping to attract more of their target 15- to 24-year-old audience.

Recent average viewing figures for popular soaps

EastEnders	11m
Coronation Street	13.5m
Neighbours	4m
Hollyoaks	2m

(BARB, 2002)

Average viewing figures in 1988

EastEnders	13.4m
Coronation Street	16.2m
Emmerdale	11.2m
Brookside	4m

(Hart, 1991)

Sponsorship

Since the 1990 Broadcasting Act, commercial television companies have been allowed to solicit sponsorship for entire programmes or series. This has enabled them to increase their revenue while reinforcing the identity of the targeted audience; a recent example possibly familiar to students is the sponsorship of *Big Brother 3* by O_2, the mobile phone company.

Sponsorship is becoming almost as important now as it was in the early days of US radio and TV soaps, when manufacturers of soap powder would advertise their products by sponsoring short dramatic spots that featured their products. These were accompanied by catchy jingles, hence the origin of the term 'soap opera', and they were aimed at the women who bought such household products and listened to the radio while they worked. Soon these spots became popular as they tended to feature the same characters in vignettes from daily life and they were expanded into dramas in their own right.

Many broadcasters are now worried that the content of programmes, and the way that the audiences view them, will be as affected by sponsorship as it is in the US. For example, American audiences can expect a (notional) half-hour programme to be interrupted two or three times by advertisements, whereas, in the UK, we would expect only one advertising break. The structure of the narratives of all programmes made for commercial broadcast is dictated by the number and length of advertising breaks, and this may be detected by careful viewing of US and UK programmes on UK television.

Until the end of 2003, the time dedicated to television advertising was regulated by the Independent Television Commission (ITC), the body responsible for maintaining standards on British independent television. This responsibility has now passed to Ofcom. The placement of products on television programmes is monitored to make sure that a sponsored show doesn't turn into an advertising slot for the sponsoring company. The ITC's codes for sponsorship and advertising (which are now on the Ofcom website) include an 'undue prominence' rule, which ensures that products are not shown extensively within a show and defines the length of an advertising break (extended in 2002).

You could get students to look at Ofcom's codes and policies for television broadcasting, at www.ofcom.org.uk, to get a sense of Ofcom's regulatory role.

See **Worksheet 1 Funding television**

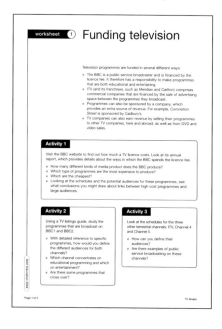
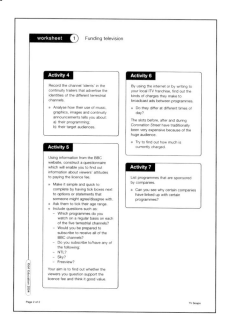

- **Scheduling**

A great deal of thought is put into the scheduling of programmes. Given the importance of advertising revenue and audience figures to the programme makers, it would not be in their interest to (for example) schedule an expensive drama aimed at adults in a daytime slot. It is the aim of the programme makers to optimise the number of viewers (to justify advertising charges or the cost to the licence fee payer). Arguably the main purpose of scheduling on commercial television is to deliver audiences to advertisers.

Consequently, when a programme is being designed, a clear target audience is established so that it can be scheduled appropriately. A cursory glance at a copy of the schedule will reveal it is split into time segments, each presuming a different audience:

- Breakfast
- Morning
- Lunchtime
- Afternoon
- Teatime/early evening
- Primetime
- Late night.

Targeting audiences

Within the segments, programme makers try to optimise the audience share they have by targeting specific audiences. During the breakfast slot, for example, the terrestrial channels broadcast a range of output. The BBC's *Breakfast News* is aimed at an older, more serious audience, while ITV's *GMTV* programme contains lighter news, more human-interest features as well as health and beauty slots. Channel 4's *RI:SE* is designed to appeal to a younger audience and features information about stars, music and fashion. Its 'hard' news content is limited, presented in a light-hearted tone and features only six items per bulletin.

The majority of the audience during the morning and afternoon slots is presumed to be female, and, because soap opera has traditionally been considered a female genre, soaps are commonly scheduled for afternoon slots. *Hollyoaks* usually appears at about 6.30pm and sits in a 'teen' slot that is covered by BBC2 and Channel 4. Programmes typically scheduled in this slot are highly successful US imports, such as *The Simpsons*, *Buffy the Vampire Slayer*, *Star Trek* and *Malcolm in the Middle*.

EastEnders and *Coronation Street* are scheduled during primetime, at either 7.30pm or 8.00pm on weekdays. This allows them to reach a wider family audience, including men. Men and women of all ages are at home by this time and have sorted out family duties, while older children have not yet gone to bed. Although competition for the primetime audience is strong, station controllers do not usually split the audience by scheduling very popular programmes head-to-head: if *EastEnders* is on the BBC at 8.00pm, *Coronation Street* is scheduled for 7.30pm.

Branding a programme also helps to draw in the audience. A programme's main signature tune generates immediate recognition with the target audience, signalling that it is time to sit down and watch. Dorothy Hobson terms this 'the siren call to view'. Although British soaps don't use music, like many television programmes, *Coronation Street* and *Hollyoaks* use brief musical 'stings' to punctuate the commercial breaks. This reinforces the brand of the soap as well as, in *Coronation Street*'s case, features the sponsor's 'spot', or product advert, and it gives the viewer time to move to or from the sofa, either for a 'comfort break' or to put the kettle on.

See **Worksheet 2 Scheduling TV soaps**

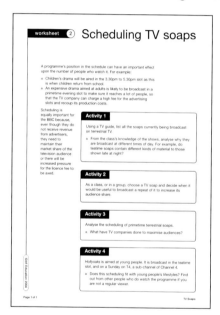

- **Quality control**

Because the channels seek to deliver a large and identifiable audience to the advertisers, there tends to be a predominance of soaps and soap hybrids, such as docusoaps and reality TV in the terrestrial and extra-terrestrial schedules. Such shows are very popular and, it is argued, provide audiences with what they want.

However, some commentators have accused television companies of 'dumbing down'. They argue that the deregulation of television in 1990 (leading to the rapid expansion of satellite TV) has led broadcasters to offer 'lowest common denominator' television to attract the mass audience – and therefore the advertisers. Docusoaps and reality TV are, with some exceptions, relatively cheap to make, as they are not dependent on stars, high production values or complex locations (and in fact are either studio-based or shot on easily accessible locations). Their popularity is often in inverse proportion to their production costs and so they are more profitable.

Nevertheless, in recent years TV soaps have been repositioned as a TV drama genre (rather than light entertainment). The two brand leaders, *Coronation Street* and *EastEnders,* vie for several annual TV acting and writing awards and are seen as an essential rite of passage for aspiring actors of stage and screen.

● Production

The production team

In overall charge of production is the **executive producer**. He or she may have several producers in their team, especially if it is a popular soap with three or four episodes per week. Producers organise the production of the programme, ensure that schedules are adhered to and all administration is taken care of. **Assistant producers** may have specific responsibility for checking continuity, making sure actors are aware of shooting schedules, etc. Each production team will be assigned a **director** who has responsibility for the way the episode is shot, while the **assistant director** will schedule filming in advance and look after health and safety issues.

Note: television producers do not tend to use the term 'genre' but 'format'; the term 'genre' has its origins in literary study and tends to be reserved for critical purposes.

The writing team

The **chief story editor** is ultimately responsible for the direction that the storyline takes, bringing ideas to the writing team at regular meetings. Once a month, or even more often, everyone involved in the creation of the story (production and writing) comes together to discuss the new ideas and decide whether they would work. A team of writers is then commissioned to write the episodes and deliver them to the **script editor** by a specified deadline. The script editor must have a thorough knowledge of the characters and projected storylines and alters the scripts as necessary to ensure consistency. A **script researcher** works with the writing team to check the authenticity of possible stories and make sure that anything medical or legal (for example) is accurately portrayed. The script then goes to the director and the production team and if accepted it is given to the actors to learn.

Key concepts

The design team

The **series designer** is in overall charge of all aspects of the production design (sets, costumes, props, make-up, etc). Designers are responsible for developing new sets and making sure that the old ones stay in good order. **Production buyers** work with the design team to buy new props, while costume designers and make-up designers ensure that the characters wear the same kinds of clothes in each episode and are made up consistently.

The technical team

There are many technical staff involved in recording a programme, including:

- Camera operators
- Lighting technicians
- Sound technicians
- Electricians.

The editing team

After the programme is filmed it must be edited to make sure the story makes sense (sequences may have been shot out of sequence) and is the right length. The **editor** works with the director and the producer to construct the final version. Sounds, like cars going past and babies crying, also need to be dubbed on.

Look at the credits for any TV programme with students to identify specific roles.

The Television Handbook, edited by Patricia Holland (1999), is an accessible guide to television production and a forthcoming title in this series, *Teaching Analysis of Television Language and Production*, also covers these technical aspects in detail.

See **Worksheet 3 Production**

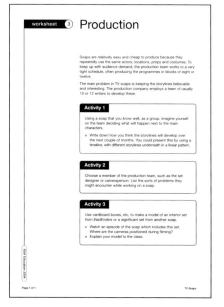

- **Publicity and promotion**

The relationship between the programme and the media is essential for maintaining programme loyalty and generating other sources of income. The **publicity department** deals with the many enquiries received from the press and television every day and ensures that the show is well promoted.

Print journalism
Local newsagents usually stock a huge array of magazines featuring the characters from the most popular soaps on their covers. The most popular, Inside Soap and All about Soap, regularly sell 250,000 and 100,000 copies per week respectively. Short articles and soap updates give information about recent events in the world of TV soap and hints (or even 'spoilers') about what might be coming up. The language tends to relate directly to the characters and plot of the soap, thus reinforcing the credibility of this world. Characters are referred to by their soap name and locations described as if they actually exist. Photographs usually feature the characters in role. Actors' names and references to the real world usually do not feature, for example a typical entry might read: '*Coronation Street*. Cold Feet. Sunita's wedding day arrives, but why is she having second thoughts?'

Such is the popularity of this kind of magazine that Granada has published a range of spin-off publications based on its two most popular soaps, *Coronation Street* and *Emmerdale*. The initial one-off magazine Emmerdale Stars celebrated the programmes 30th anniversary with a print run of 250,000. Women's magazines, such as Woman and Woman's Own, regularly feature information on TV soaps, as do teen magazines, such as Bliss and 17. Articles and 'snippets' comment on events and characters, but also provide gossip about the actors, their relationships and their work.

The internet
Because of their popularity, BBC, ITV and Channel 4 all provide lavishly designed sites for their soap operas, packed with up-to-date and detailed information. They contain a wide range of material including:

- Updates
- Character information
- Games and screensavers
- Photos
- Backstage information
- Interactivity (voting, chat rooms, competitions).

There are also numerous fan sites.

Television

The programmes are also promoted heavily on television, and the new digital channels are important in this process. The BBC has developed a spin-off series, usually restricted to BBC3, called *EastEnders Revealed*. It features all kinds of extra information on the soap, together with extracts from favourite episodes, which tend to feature specific characters or storylines over a period of time, thus reinforcing its own popularity, treating fans to more of their favourite programme, and maintaining its flagship status. In order to publicise its new digital channel, the BBC screened the next day's episode of *EastEnders* on BBC3 straight after BBC1's daily episode, so fans did not have to wait a day to see what happened next, and a repeat of the day's episode of *EastEnders* is scheduled at 10pm on BBC3. ITV's partner digital channel, ITV2, shows repeats of *Coronation Street*. Both programmes have weekend omnibus editions.

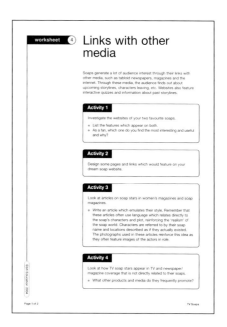

See **Worksheet 4 Links with other media**

Forms and conventions

Although current soap operas may appear to address very modern issues and provide interactive games and chat online for avid fans on the internet, the structure and concerns of modern soaps are fundamentally the same as those of the original soaps.

This section addresses the following questions:

- Where did soap operas originate?
- What is the history of British soaps?
- What kind of themes, characters and settings can we expect to find in TV soaps?
- What kind of narrative structure is associated with soap operas?
- How is realism constructed in TV soaps?
- What do we call programmes that are like soaps but that don't quite fit the generic characteristics?

- **History**

The term 'soap opera' was originally applied to radio drama serials broadcast in America during the 1930s and 40s. This was as a result of commercial sponsorship of the programmes by manufacturers of washing powder, other cleaning products, health products and foods. The serials, which were extremely popular with housewives, provided a ready-made target audience for companies such as Procter and Gamble, Colgate-Palmolive and Pillsbury to market their products, and played an important role in the commercial success of these companies in the first half of the 20th century.

Early US soap operas

- The first soap opera was born when the manager of the Chicago radio station WGN approached a detergent company in 1930 with the idea of a daily, serialised drama in which the two central characters were a mother and her daughter. It was called *Painted Dreams* and was written by Irna Phillips, who then made her name in writing radio soap operas.
- The narrative format of *Painted Dreams* and subsequent soaps was rooted in the tradition of the popular serialised novels for women published in the 19th century and the serialised stories published in women's magazines in the 1920s and 30s.
- The format was adopted by early commercial radio broadcasters as they experimented with new forms of programming in an attempt to find out what attracted audiences and, therefore, advertisers.
- Most radio soaps in the US at this time were produced by advertising companies on behalf of their clients.
- Although comedy serials had been popular in the 1920s, these serialised domestic dramas were the first to be aimed specifically at women and broadcast in the afternoon. The serial form became increasingly popular in America during the 1930s and between 1933 and 1937 serial dramas became the staple of daytime programming (Robert C Allen, 1995).
- By 1941 serials represented nearly 90% of all advertiser-sponsored daytime programming in the US.
- The popularity of soaps continued into the 1950s with the introduction of television and the form transferred easily.

See **Worksheet 5 History of TV soaps**

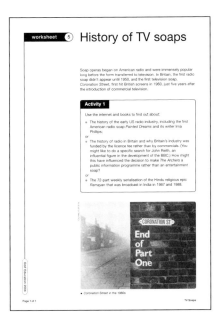

Key concepts

Key concepts

- **British soap opera**

Soap opera has also played an important role in the history of British television and radio.

- *The Archers* was first broadcast on radio in 1950 by the BBC. This daily 15-minute serial was intended to educate farmers about agricultural practices. It is still running, with regular audiences of just under five million, and still features current concerns of the agricultural community, such as rural theft, organic farming, government subsidies and foot and mouth disease.
- The first television soap, *The Grove Family*, appeared on BBC1 in 1954, just before the introduction of commercial television in this country in 1955. *Coronation Street* was first broadcast in 1960, originally only to viewers receiving output from the Manchester-based Granada franchise. Within a year the programme went national and it has remained one of Britain's most popular programmes, with current audiences of around 13 million.
- The *Street*'s style was gritty and urban; it reflected the 'angry young man' movement that had influenced literature, drama and film throughout the late 1950s and early 1960s.
- British soap operas are characterised by their predominantly urban identities (*Emmerdale*, set in the Yorkshire Dales, is the rural exception), including *Crossroads*, set near Birmingham (1964–88, then 2001–3), *Brookside*, set in Liverpool (1982–2003), *EastEnders*, set in east London (1985–present) and *Hollyoaks*, set in Chester (1995–present). This has been an important factor in establishing the social realism of British soaps (see page 34).
- The most popular Welsh-language television programme is a soap, *Pobol Y Cwm* (*People of the Valley*) and is shown on the Welsh-language channel, S4C.
- In Britain, TV soaps are an enduring popular cultural form and regularly top the television ratings. They also span the schedule dominating the afternoon, teatime and early evening slots.

See **Worksheet 6 British soap and social realism**

1 of 2 pages

- **International soap**

The soap opera genre is just as important to international audiences. In Latin America for example, *telenovelas* dominate the primetime schedules and the serials are exported to countries all over the world. The most popular television programme in China in 1991 was *Kewang* (*Yearnings* or *Expectations*), which was, according to The Washington Post, 'the biggest hit on television in Chinese history'. The 72-part weekly serialisation of the Hindu religious epic *Ramayan*, broadcast in India between 1987–8, was regularly watched by 80 to 100 million people.

The US has had a plethora of successful television soaps, dominated by the long-running, and arguably iconic, *Dallas* and *Dynasty* in the 1980s and 1990s. There is not space here to do justice to the many and diverse TV soaps from the US, many of which have been very popular in the UK. In contrast to British soap operas these did not have their origins in social realism; their trademark was a powerful combination of escapist fantasy and unadulterated glamour, luxury, greed and sex. These features proved at odds with the global recession of the 1990s and storylines grew increasingly incredible, resulting in the loss of audiences at home and abroad.

Today, the US soap, as seen in the UK, has been supplanted in its popularity by US sitcoms, such as *Friends*, *Will & Grace*, *The Simpsons* and *Frasier*, or adult drama series, such as *Sex and the City*, *Ally McBeal*, the long-running hospital drama, *ER*, and a slew of impressive imports, such as *24* and *Six Feet Under*. Nevertheless, several US daytime soaps are currently shown on satellite/cable/digital channels in the UK.

- **Generic characteristics**

The idea of genre is important for audiences as it allows them to categorise entertainment forms to help them make choices about the kind of programmes or films they prefer to watch at any particular time.

Categorising a media product into a genre (or format) also makes it easier for producers to target particular audiences because they have ideas about what different kinds of audiences like and, more importantly, as we have seen above, they know how they can schedule it and sell it to advertisers.

In a critical context, genres are analysed in terms of their codes and conventions, the typical creative constituents that have become associated with a particular genre. These include recurring themes, archetypal characters, typical settings and locations, and the use of *mise en scène*, moving image language, stylistic motifs and narrative elements and structure.

It is important that students appreciate that genres are not governed by fixed rules, but are forms that change over time and can develop into hybrids in

Key concepts

order to avoid becoming predictable and losing their audience. The soap genre in the UK is a broad and varied one, with some soaps employing characters in a comic mode more associated with situation comedy (as occasionally seen in *Coronation Street* and *Emmerdale*). Other soaps can use performance and a visual style that relate more to documentary or crime drama (as seen in early and current episodes of *EastEnders* and occasionally in *Brookside*). Predictability can also be avoided as producers can choose to experiment or deviate from established narrative or stylistic conventions.

In recent years, *EastEnders* in particular, has experimented with visual conventions borrowed from film, such as extravagant crane shots for overheads of characters in crisis, isolated against their setting (and very occasionally slow motion editing and even a flashback in one instance, to Phil Mitchell's childhood). This programme has also freely departed from the narrative convention, used by most soaps, of each episode beginning with the start of a new day. During especially intense storylines, two or more episodes might be split by a minute, in narrative terms, in order to maintain the atmosphere of the piece and the concentration and involvement of the audience.

Retaining an audience for a popular genre is always a careful balance between the comfort experienced in the recognition and repetition of familiar elements and the occasional surprise or shock, or violation of expectation, that keeps the viewer engaged, and successful soaps employ both tactics.

Themes

In *Media and Meaning – An Introduction*, Stewart *et al* (2001) identify a number of common themes in the soap narrative:

- Love
- Conflict
- Secrets and confidences
- Sickness and injury
- Skeletons in the cupboard
- Plans going wrong.

Two additional important themes, particularly in *EastEnders* and *Neighbours*, are family feuds and family loyalty.

Themes are controlling ideas that exist in narratives and, in soap storylines, they explore dominant features of our daily lives. In this way, they show audiences experiences with which, at some level, they can identify, even if they do not share the setting or social class of a soap character.

Thus the strong identification a viewer might feel with a soap is rather less to do with where it is set or who is in it and more to do with the situations depicted because the conflicts and dilemmas that the characters face are, to some degree (and excepting scriptwriters' more imaginative flights of fancy), ones that we all face from time to time, regardless of cultural or social differences. It could be said that the concentrated emotional intensity and frequency of dramatic occurrences (such as illness, death, adultery etc) in soaps give us opportunities to rehearse what we would do in a particular situation or provide us a cathartic release.

The fact that soap themes are rooted in daily life also affords the viewer ample opportunity to comment and judge the actions of others (or the *Schadenfreude* of plain old-fashioned gossip!). Also, the viewer can enjoy a narrative omniscience that is not shared by the characters on screen and the resulting effect, of dramatic irony, is a classic dramatic device for engaging an audience. These aspects of audience study will be discussed in greater detail under Narrative pleasures (page 31), Realism (see page 32) and Audience (page 36).

Melodrama

Soap is characterised by elements of melodrama, in its focus on family issues and its use of dramatic irony, romantic plots and heightened emotionality. It also relies heavily on dramatic cliff-hangers, intense close-ups and family occasions, such as weddings, which act as sites of conflict rather than of narrative unity or closure.

Like film melodrama, TV soap opera is generally regarded as a female genre, and has been derided for its lack of seriousness and emotional triteness. However, in recent years British soap opera has been taken more seriously as a dramatic form, which combines melodrama with social realism and classic realist style.

(See page 43 for a fuller discussion on soap opera as a gendered genre.)

Characters

Central to TV soaps is the concept of community. The storylines rely heavily on the characters knowing each other; they all live or work together and care about each other's activities and business. Although this idea has been criticised by many people as being unrealistic and unrepresentative of modern society, it is key to the way the genre works.

Consequently, the characters are often related to each other or are very closely linked for other social reasons (or at the least, geographical ones). The key social group is the family, which is the basis for most relationships between characters. This places women, given their traditional role at the heart of the family, centre stage. The strong matriarchal figure, as seen in characters past and present, such as Elsie Tanner, Lou Beale, Pauline Fowler and Deidre Barlow, is a classic feature of the genre and responsible in part for its continued success.

Jordan (in Dyer, 1981) identifies further character types in *Coronation Street*:

- Grandmother figures
- Marriageable characters (men and women)
- Married couples
- Rogues.

David Buckingham (1987) identifies the following stereotypes in *EastEnders*:

- The gossip
- The bastard
- The tart.

And Peter Buckman (1985) adds:

- The decent husband
- The good woman
- The villain
- The bitch.

Some of these archetypes can be identified in all TV soaps. However, while some characters remain as types, other characters are more fully developed. For example, in *EastEnders*, Graham, the villain who raped Mo Mitchell, is unlikely to be developed beyond the stereotype. Dennis Rickman (Den Watt's illegitimate son), is also a villain, but occasionally is a hero and love interest; he is of far more interest to the audience who may even identify with him at times. While Graham is a transient character and therefore more two-dimensional, Dennis offers the 'intimate familiarity' (Dorothy Hobson, 2003) of the character who is well known to the audience and over time has become multilayered and complex.

Settings

All soaps are set in recognisable environments which contain a limited number of sets that the audience are familiar with. This may be a small community, a street or even a place of work. *Neighbours* is set in Ramsay Street specifically, and more widely in the suburb of Erinsborough in Australia. *EastEnders* is located in Walford (a fictional place in east London), and more specifically, Albert Square. In and around Albert Square, the audience are led to believe, are places the characters live and regularly visit. Narrative action rarely takes place outside the community, although other real places are referred to, such as Melbourne, or the West End of London (always 'up West' in *EastEnders'* argot!) in order to imbue credibility.

The focus on a clearly defined community may be one of TV soap opera's main attractions. Many TV soaps hark back to a mythical golden age when everybody knew each other and left their doors open. A long-running soap is familiar to its audience, and may provide the sense of security that lies in being somewhere that you know well. Christine Geraghty (1991), in discussing 'soap space', suggests that, in theory, a TV soap could run forever. The programme writers need to make the environment a familiar and pleasurable space to revisit. The fact that the audience knows the community intimately becomes a source of pleasure. This familiarity means that audiences find it easy to pick up narrative threads even after missing a number of episodes.

- **Narrative pleasures**
  - Soap opera uses an open-ended narrative structure; there is no formal closure at the end of each episode. Feminist theorists argue that soaps offer a feminised narrative structure, in contrast to a masculinised narrative characterised by the drive towards formal closure. This further supports the idea that soap offers special space to women viewers (see page 41).
  - To keep the audience hooked, so they return next time, there is usually a cliff-hanger at the end of each episode. This has become such a familiar convention that some soaps like *Hollyoaks* use the cliff-hanger as an ironic comment on the programme (see Case study 4). In generating a sense of expectation, the soap also becomes a feature of social interaction and discussion between each episode, which enhances the pleasure of watching.
  - Another source of audience pleasure is the equilibrium between the community and the individual characters. This is created by the way the writers can interweave or link together several separate storylines (a multistranded narrative) because they all occur in one place.
  - TV soap has a very complex narrative structure and requires a great deal of commitment from the audience to keep up with developments (many fans will insist that an episode is video taped if they're away or out, for example). This investment by the audience is an important contributor to their loyalty.

- **When is a soap not a soap?**

Many programmes contain similar structural elements but do not fit into the soap category. Soap-style characteristics of programmes like *The Bill*, *Casualty* and *ER* are:

- The same main characters are used in every episode;
- The same locations are used in every episode.

But they differ too:

- Each programme can be viewed in isolation. The audience have the satisfaction of closure;
- All three of these dramas feature characters that appear for only one episode; their problems or illness are resolved or passed on to other professionals by the end of the programme;

Key concepts

- Generally these programmes last longer than the average soap, cost a lot more to produce and have prominent positions in the schedules;
- They tend to run in series for a season and then return after a break.

Docusoap (as seen in early examples, such as *Airport*, *Vets in Practice* and *The Cruise*) is a relatively new genre in which each programme returns to the same setting every time but uses real people and real places as the focus for the action, rather than fictional ones. Reality TV programmes such as *Big Brother*, *Fame Academy*, *Pop Idol* and *I'm a Celebrity – Get Me out of Here!* bear many hallmarks of the soap, but their use of real rather than fictional characters and settings sets them apart from soap opera. They are generic hybrids, in that they also owe a great deal to the game show and fly-on-the-wall documentary.

They rarely achieve audience figures as high as the soaps and are unlikely to gain similar popularity, some subsequent series having recently slumped in the ratings: 'People playing themselves playing up to television is not the same as a fantastically written character in a soap.' (Suzanne Moore, *The Soap Opera: Fiction or Reality*, BBC2, 1999). Nevertheless this hybrid offers ample opportunities for successive series, re-runs, companion coverage on digital/cable/satellite channels, such as ITV2, BBC 3 and E4, as well as international franchises, for example, *American Idol*.

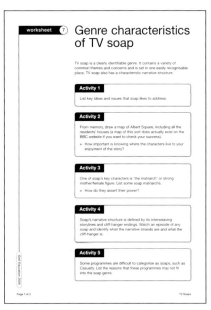

See **Worksheet 7**
Genre characteristics of TV soap

1 of 2 pages

- **Realism and ideology**

> There is no realism, but there are realisms. (John Ellis, *Visible Fictions*, 1982)

Arguing about whether a TV soap is realistic is not that useful an exercise. However, debating the ways in which realism is constructed in soaps will equip students with the necessary tools to write about this complex subject. Realism is a problematic, and relative concept, which continues to be debated in the academic world, and students should be encouraged to consider these complexities.

The above quotation makes it clear that there are a number of different ways of constructing realism, which will depend on different cultures and contexts. The construction of realism in film and media is governed by a set of aesthetic codes and conventions which change over time. In addition, realist media texts need to employ an ideological realism, with ideas, values and beliefs which are represented as believable and convincing to an audience, even if not shared by them. One of the best ways to illustrate this to students is to show them extracts from early episodes of *Coronation Street* and compare them with contemporary extracts, using the theory below to aid discussion.

O'Sullivan, Dutton and Rayner (1998) identified four features of the construction of realism in media texts:

- **Surface realism**: The scene that the soap (or any other programme) is revealing to the audience has to be accurately presented. In the same way that an audience would expect a drama set in 1850 to use props and sets that are appropriate to the period, the soap audience expects the scene to look 'real' and have a strong sense of verisimilitude. Costumes are likely to be contemporary and reflect the type of person the character is. Props, such as cars and domestic appliances, should be up-to-date. Buildings have to be specific to the location (for example, back-to-back terraces in Manchester in *Coronation Street*) and interior sets in accordance with the character who lives there. Soaps also try to replicate real time in that events that take place in consecutive episodes will happen consecutively within the narrative. For example, Thursday's episode of *EastEnders* may allude to the fact that it is indeed Thursday in the plot, and Monday's episode may refer to events that have happened to the characters over the weekend away from the audience.
- **Emotional realism**: Ien Ang (1985), discussing the US soap *Dallas*, argued that despite the unrealistic plotlines and actions, the audience, on the whole, found that they could identify with the psychology and share the feelings of the characters. This emotional realism meant that the audience enjoyed watching the soap. Emotional realism allows us to understand why Lisa shot Phil in *EastEnders*, and how Sonia felt when she found out she was being two-timed by Jamie. It is also important that the characters do not 'act out of character' as this undermines the programme's realism.
- **Plausible plots**: When a plane crashed into Emmerdale, killing quite a large proportion of the characters, some of the audience saw this as very far-fetched and stopped watching the soap. Some commentators argue that *Brookside* ultimately failed because its plots became increasingly implausible. Audiences need to be able to believe that what happens in a soap might (just) happen in real life.
- **Technical and symbolic codes**: This refers to the way the audience expect the soap to be presented to them. For example, most TV soaps

utilise a classic realist style of filming, meaning that the editing employed makes the cutting between shots and scenes largely invisible. A TV soap which suddenly switched to a documentary style of filming and used long takes or handheld cameras, for example, would make the audience feel uncomfortable and put them off. Although it has been the subject of pastiche or parody by many comedy programmes and cultural commentators, the final shocked stare of a character at the end of an episode is so much part of the coding of the soap genre, it is not questioned by the audience (although see the section on cliff-hangers in Case study 4 on *Hollyoaks*).

Social realism

British soaps owe a great deal to the social realist tradition in film and literature, using a style and approach which relates to the 'angry young man' or 'kitchen sink' drama movements of the 1950s and 60s. This movement was characterised by the work of John Osborne, seminally, in his 1956 play *Look Back in Anger*.

The soap opera form also undoubtedly owes much to Charles Dickens and Thomas Hardy, whose serialised novels (sold in weekly magazine publications) contained some of the recognisable prototypical elements of a soap, albeit in literary form, such as strong melodramatic and multi-stranded narratives, character archetypes and realistic quotidian settings. They also had a strong desire to tackle important issues of the day, such as poverty, unemployment, disease, adultery, illegitimate children, and commanded the loyalty of an enthusiastic popular audience, as well as a critical one.

In post-World War II Britain, some filmmakers and writers focused on issues of working- and lower middle-class life, poverty and youth as subjects for their work. Social realist films and dramas used young and working-class actors and actual locations.

A number of successful young writers from the north of England set their dramas in cities such as:

- Bradford (*Room at the Top* – novel by John Braine, film directed by Jack Clayton, 1959);
- Nottingham (*A Kind of Loving* – novel by Stan Barstow, film directed by John Schlesinger, 1962);
- Salford (*A Taste of Honey* – play by Shelagh Delaney, film directed by Tony Richardson, 1961).

To some degree, TV soaps such as *EastEnders* and *Coronation Street* sought to emulate this approach by using young and working-class actors, trying to replicate an authentic working-class environment in their sets, accents and dialect and by addressing contemporary social issues. For example, HIV, disability and domestic violence have all featured in popular British soaps in recent years. However, both soaps now have a broader class profile than originally, perhaps in an attempt to attract a wider audience, or in order to reflect the blurring between definitions of working – and middle-class status in contemporary British society.

Limits of realism

However, it is important to remind students that all television material is mediated; it is not a mirror of the real world, but represents a specific view of the world.

Stewart *et al* (2001) has put forward the following criticisms of the construction of realism of soap and its representations:

- Problems that characters face may not be linked to the wider world. For example, a character may experience unemployment, but instead of linking this to wider social trends, the programme may concentrate upon individual circumstances. This means that the problem is seen as limited to the individual and not related to the public or political sphere.
- It is also often claimed that minority characters are misrepresented or under-represented. Some British soaps, for example, do not feature characters of colour or anyone from a differing ethnic or religious background. If we increasingly see British Asian and Afro-Caribbean characters, we rarely see Greek or Chinese characters although both groups represent thriving minority communities in Britain.
- We rarely see characters do mundane day-to-day routine work, such as housework (although this tends to be true of all realist drama).
- Soaps can be very moralistic. Characters who step out of line, through infidelity or crime, for example, are often punished (at least by getting their 'just deserts' in the storyline).
- Owing to their production schedules and advance filming of episodes, most soaps cannot reflect contemporary news events, no matter how significant. Thus, events like 11 September 2001 never reach Weatherfield or Albert Square and so the realism portrayed can only ever be a 'surface reality'.

Soap opera can be seen as quite a reactionary form. For example, while soaps reinforce the notion of community and offer reassuring security, as discussed above, they tend to support the *status quo*, and opportunities for change and personal advancement are limited. This reactionary nature is also governed by a formal consideration: owing to the restricted location of soaps' production, the main characters can never develop in significant ways, or advance themselves, as to do so, they would inevitably have to leave home, and hence the series. Soap production and narrative conventions mean that the genre never follows characters, except for temporary excursions, such as holidays.

However, other commentators argue that it can still be seen as a progressive genre because the feminised narrative structure allows space for a range of interpretations in its representations of women. But the increasing number of more rounded male characters in modern soaps, and the more varied roles they now play, and the growth of a mixed age and gender audience, means that this view is open to debate and would be a useful research study.

See **Worksheet 8 Realism and reality**

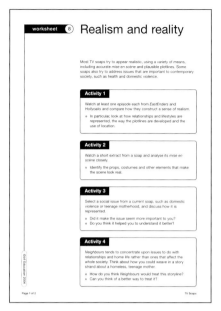

1 of 2 pages

Audiences

• Media effects

A central consideration for students is whether the media influences our behaviour and how we think. This issue has been hotly debated and approaches to assessing the process and levels of effect have changed over time as opinions about the media have changed. Because the genre plays such an important role in the cultural life of so many people, students of TV soap opera have to consider their impact on society and the degree to which they represent it in a 'realistic' way.

This section will cover the following questions:

- How and to what extent are audiences influenced by the behaviour of the characters in, or the content, of soaps?
- How do audiences watch and use soaps, eg, for diversion, or to get advice about an event in their own life?
- Can soaps have more influence over people's behaviour and opinions than actual experience?

• Summary of theories

Several of the key theories relating to the discussion about audience effects are summarised below. In fact the theories, and the way they relate to each other, are more complex than this chronological presentation implies, as a number of the ideas and presumptions underlying them continue to be influential and debated. In the following section these theories are applied to a consideration of the audience effects of TV soaps.

The hypodermic model

Some early theorists in audience research argued that we should be concerned about the consequences of the mass media's ability to reach large numbers of people. Rooted in a view of the masses as uneducated and therefore essentially passive in their reception of propaganda, a moral panic arose in the early decades of the 20th century that increases in violence and crime were a result of the representation of these behaviours in the vastly popular new 'picture houses'.

Some theorists conceptualised these fears in terms of a hypodermic syringe, depicting a process whereby media messages about acceptable or challenging behaviour, for example, were 'injected' into the audience. They presented individuals as having no control over the effect of the message on themselves, and essentially being victims of the manipulations of producers or controllers of the media. While this view has been generally discredited in academic circles, it is still voiced today when, for example, a fresh wave of concern over screen violence explodes in the newspapers.

The two-step flow model

By the 1940s and 50s views about the power of the media had been modified, largely as a result of *Personal Influence*, a study of voting behaviour and the influence of political persuasion by Katz and Lazarsfeld in 1955. They found that instead of the media being all powerful, audience opinion was much more likely to be affected by important people, 'opinion leaders', in their social spheres. They argued that media influence occurred in two steps, with a media message's influence on audiences depending on how it was interpreted and discussed by their political and community leaders.

Uses and gratifications – audience-centred study

Sociology and psychology theorists in the 1970s developed a more audience-centred view which asked about the role that audiences themselves played in the effects of the media. For example, in his study of the television-watching audience, James Lull (1990) put forward a comprehensive list of audience uses and gratifications, including companionship, structuring the day, communication, problem-solving, and behaviour modelling.

McQuail, Blumler and Brown (1972) defined four main categories of need that the media gratifies:

- Diversion – a form of escape and emotional release;
- Personal relationships – from companionship of the medium and discussion of it afterwards with friends and family;

- Personal identity – the exploration of personal problems through soap characters and the reinforcement of our roles and values through comparison;
- Surveillance – information about the world.

This view highlights the receiver of the message rather than the sender and represents the viewer/reader as active rather than passive.

● TV soap – a peril or a pleasure?

So how have these theories influenced discussions about soap audiences? Critics have tended to dismiss the genre as mass-produced pulp, churned out to cater for popular tastes, which could only do harm to authentic art and culture.

As Robert C Allen points out:

> With a few notable exceptions, the television critic writing in magazines and newspapers has shown as much interest in writing about soap opera as the restaurant critic has in writing about McDonald's – and for much the same reason: they are both regarded as 'junk'. (1995, p5)

Warning – soaps can damage your health

So strong were the anti-soap feelings in its early days that a New York psychiatrist, Louis Berg, stated that listening to soap was responsible for a multitude of illnesses and maladies: 'emotional and physical disturbances, ranging from gastrointestinal distress to nocturnal fright' (Allen, 1995, p5). Although these statements were not backed by any scientific research, Berg's attitude and approach fitted neatly with the prevailing views in academic and political circles of the mass media at the time. TV soap, like many of the other popular new entertainment forms such as cinema, was, in this view, dangerous for your health and should be treated with caution.

Although these views seem extreme today, a recent report by the Broadcasting Standards Commission, *Soap Box or Soft Soap* (May 2002), argued that the desire to raise audience figures has led to increasingly aggressive themes in soaps. Violent scenes in *EastEnders* and *Coronation Street* were singled out as particular cause for concern, as their pre-watershed scheduling slots meant that they could be seen by children. This indicates that the commission feels that violent programmes do have an effect on younger viewers. One person in eight interviewed from a sample of 2,000 for the report felt that soaps were inappropriate for children.

This has led to Education Secretary Charles Clarke demanding a meeting with broadcasters to discuss the findings. (See Case study 1 on *EastEnders*.) In addition, there is concern about the number of scenes shot in pubs in British soaps and discussion of whether this could be limited in order to discourage alcoholism and violence induced by alcohol.

- Students could use the internet to research the debate on violence in TV soaps.

American studies of the 1940s and 50s were less concerned with the direct effects of soaps than with the way that audiences used the genre. As Allen outlines, the conclusions of these studies were rarely positive and generally reinforced the patriarchal attitudes of American society of the time. They categorised a typical viewer as 'a woman suffering from some deficiency – whether emotional, psychological, social, relational, or some combination of them all' (Allen, 1995, p6), who used the medium to help resolve their problems.

More pleasure than pain
Some critics are still derogatory of TV soap and regard it as a female genre. However, feminist theorists of the 1970s and 80s took a very different view and helped to improve the status of the genre as legitimate academic study. Dorothy Hobson (1982) argued that soap evoked different meanings and pleasures for different audiences. Allen pointed out that pleasures and meanings are 'deeply imbedded [sic] in the social contexts of their viewing' and

> Crossroads is a very different experience for a young mother who feeds her child while she watches than for the widowed grandmother who views alone. (1995, p9)

David Buckingham's study of *EastEnders* (1987) concludes from extensive audience research that young people and children do not passively absorb information from soaps. Interviewees were aware of constructed messages and were appropriately critical of the views and ideas the programme put forward.

Richard Kilborn (1992) suggests that audiences watch TV soaps because they are:

- A regular part of domestic routine and entertaining reward for work;
- A launch pad for social and personal interaction;
- A fulfilment of individual needs: a way of choosing to be alone or enduring enforced loneliness;
- Escapist fantasies;
- A focus for debate on topical issues.

Watching soaps also leads to:

- Involvement and identification with characters;
- A kind of critical game that involves knowledge of the rules and conventions of the genre.

Key concepts

Because TV soap opera is such a popular genre, the behaviour of soap audiences has become a focus for research, particularly in Media and Cultural Studies.

See **Worksheet 9 Effects theories**

- **Active fan behaviour**

The fact that so many people buy magazines like *TV Soap* and visit websites dedicated to TV soaps shows that many people are highly active fans of the programmes. Fans take pleasure in following the storylines and characters of soaps, so the main TV channels have developed special websites for all their soap operas in order to allow fans to access more detailed information about the programmes and their favourite stars. There are also websites produced independently by the fans themselves; a good example is www.perfectblend.net, which has many useful articles on *Neighbours*.

1 of 2 pages

Many soap stars have their own devoted fan clubs and there is a tradition of soap stars attempting to cross into the music industry and other entertainment forms, following their 'soap' career. Martine McCutcheon and Kylie Minogue are just two examples of performers whose singing careers took off as a result of their roles in soaps. Producers also use fan interest, in particular, stars as a way of drawing attention to their soaps, for example by casting familiar and iconic actors such as Barbara Windsor in the role of Peggy Mitchell in *EastEnders*.

See **Worksheet 10 Fans**

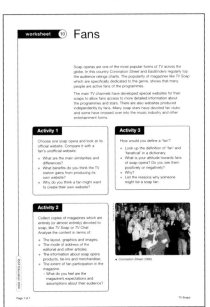

- **Who watches TV soaps?**

Christine Geraghty (1991) suggests that the 1980s saw the TV soap opera gaining in recognition due to two emerging trends: a growing interest in popular culture, and a new respect for feminist theory and its insights into media texts. This led to a re-examination of the role and identity of what had previously been dismissed by critics as a 'women's genre'.

Geraghty writes:

> The impact of feminism has been critical in creating an atmosphere in which the traditional skills and pleasures assigned to women could be re-evaluated rather than dismissed; this reassessment covered a range of cultural issues, from the apparently frivolous, such as the role of fashion and dress in women's lives to the more obviously serious … In this changing atmosphere it became possible to acknowledge the pleasures of soap opera and to argue that soaps are not inherently worthless but have been made to seem so. (1991, p2)

She concluded that four elements helped to explain why TV soap (and other women's genres such as romance) had such strong appeal for women. The factors were:

- A central female character with whom the audience are encouraged to identify;
- An acknowledgment of the importance of the domestic sphere in people's lives;
- An emphasis on the importance of relationships;
- The privileging of fantasy linked to the private sphere.

Dorothy Hobson (1982) pointed out that watching *Crossroads* gave the female viewer a 'cultural space' which they could claim as their own.

Buckingham's study (1987) of the audience for *EastEnders* found that many young people and children watched the programme. There is a popular belief that men are more interested in action genres and the public sphere, and that they resist watching more 'female' genres such as soaps. However, the reality is that men now make up a significant part of the audience for TV soaps, although they may be less prepared to admit to it, because of its low cultural status or association with female viewing preferences. Soaps like *EastEnders* have made a point of targeting a male audience with their storylines in order to broaden their mainstream appeal, and youth soaps like *Hollyoaks* have aimed to develop both their male and female characters equally.

See **Worksheets 11 and 13 Who watches TV soaps?** (on the following page)

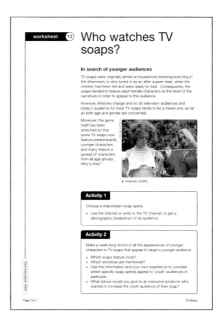

Representation and ideology

All media texts present a view of the world which more or less accords with an agenda set by the organisation that is broadcasting or printing the medium. When analysing any media text we must ask 'Whose view is it?' and 'What messages are they sending about the world?' The following questions are considered:

- To what extent do soaps reflect real people in terms of gender, class, age and racial/regional representations and to what extent are the characters little more than stereotypes?
- Whose viewpoint are stereotype characters in soaps representing?
- Are the messages produced by the media deliberately encoded in the soaps to influence us or do they reflect the attitudes of real people?
- What have theorists said about this process?

• Stereotypes and archetypes

Branston and Stafford (2001) argue that because soaps show stories with a universal appeal about families and communities they rely heavily on 'archetypal characters' and use stereotypes to ensure ready accessibility to the casual viewer. Archetypal characters have existed throughout the history of the narrative form and include heroes and villains, earth mothers and prodigal sons, vamps and victims. Stereotypes are more specific to cultural and historical trends.

> Stereotypes depend on shared cultural knowledge and to this extent some part of the stereotypical image must "ring true" for most people. (Branston and Stafford, 2001)

Stereotypes are composite images which emphasise certain common features about distinctive groups of people. These are not always negative, and they help to make stories more immediately accessible because they are based on commonly shared assumptions about people. However, while characters, when they are first introduced, tend to be stereotyped, over time they usually become more individualised.

- Students could identify some main characters from TV soaps and some less important characters and discuss to what extent the representation of these characters is complex or stereotypical.

● Gender

A place for powerful women?

Since the 1970s, feminists have criticised the way that women have been stereotyped on television, in both programmes and advertising. Until recently, they were most often stereotyped either in the role of housewife and carer, or as pretty and sexually attractive. As a 'women's genre', soaps have tended to offer more complex representations of women. As Mike Clarke points out:

> Soaps are almost the only television programmes which allow women who do not fit the stereotypes of slim, youthful beauty to have a romantic or sexual existence (1987).

It would be very useful to discuss this quote with students to see whether the same can be said of popular television over 15 years later.

In *Neighbours* all the female characters have roles outside the home, including vicar, headmistress, nurse, hairdresser, journalist and lawyer. However, these characters have less depth than the female characters in the evening soaps and promote a somewhat idealised view of the world. (See Case study 2 on *Neighbours*.)

While most soaps do offer strong and quite complex women characters, because the genre focuses on families and closed communities, women's roles in the home tend to predominate, with many of them still placing woman as the carer. Jaquetta May, who played feminist lecturer Rachel in *EastEnders*, argues that women in soaps are limited in the degree of their economic success. The more successful they are professionally, the more likely they are to leave the community – and be written out of the soap. *Coronation Street* writer Darren Little agrees:

> Rita is the wealthiest person on Coronation Street. I'm constantly trying to find ways for her to lose her money. (*Woman's Hour*, Radio 4, 22 April 2002)

Stereotyped men

Because of the strong focus on the domestic sphere and 'women's concerns' in soaps, it could be argued that the male characters are more likely to suffer from stereotyping. For example, Jack Duckworth fulfils the function of the henpecked husband in *Coronation Street*. While there are powerful men in soaps, in part to help attract male viewers, the qualities we associate with femininity are privileged and the male characters have to conform to these.

We had sympathy for Grant and Phil Mitchell in *EastEnders*, despite their thug-stud status, because they were capable of displaying sensitivity and emotional trauma. In contrast, Nick Cotton (Dot's son) was unable to express emotion and betrayed his own mother; this violated one of the core values of the soap community and as a result he fulfilled the role of the archetypal villain. Interestingly, Australian soaps are remarkable for their representations of the romances and sexual relationships between older men and women, which might indicate the demographics of their audience.

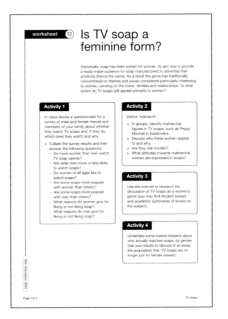

Representations of gender in soaps are therefore far from straightforward and offer rich material for debate in the classroom.

See **Worksheet 12 Is TV soap a feminine form?**

● Class and community

Most British soaps focus on characters who are mainly working class. The subject matter of soap opera means that these characters spend their time arguing with the neighbours, fighting, or having affairs. While this overall portrayal of working-class life may not be entirely accurate, individual characterisations are complex and generally quite positive. (See Case study 1 on *EastEnders*.)

However, both *EastEnders* and *Coronation Street* have been criticised for their unrealistic representations of family and community, harking back to a past time when community spirit was much stronger, everybody knew each other and the extended family relationship was the norm (see pages 52ff and 73ff). Research has found that for some people the security of the soap community replaces a lack in their own community or family relationships, and this is one of the reasons behind soaps' continuing popularity.

However, for all the emphasis on family and 'sticking together', families in soaps frequently argue and betray each other, sometimes spectacularly, so the rhetoric of characters' dialogue is often at odds with the reality of their actions. Is this also a reflection of our own lives, in that we do not always manage to live up to our own principles and expectations? The recognisable fallibility, then, of soap characters is another aspect of their appeal.

See **Worksheet 14 Representations of family and community**

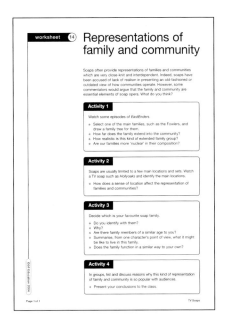

- ## Race

Many critics point out that ethnic minorities are under-represented in TV soaps. Until very recently *Coronation Street* had no non-white characters, despite Manchester and its surrounding areas being home to an enormous British Asian population. When new British Asian characters were introduced into the soap, the writers of the programme chose to reflect the stereotype of British Asians as corner shop owners. *Neighbours* rarely features any ethnic characters, despite some parts of Australia being home to large Asian and Greek populations, and therefore constituting a significant percentage of a potential audience.

Current episodes of *EastEnders* and *Coronation Street* though, would be excellent texts for the study of representation of race.

See **Worksheet 15 Stereotyping and representations**

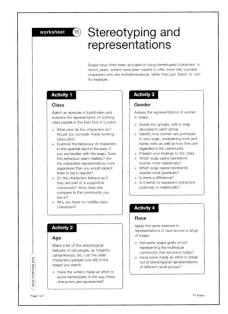

• Messages and values

'Soaps turn to healthy plotlines' was a headline in The Observer, 28 December 2003. The article indicated that the government believes it can convey ideological messages more effectively though soaps than through other forms of media and has held talks with broadcasters to discuss ways of using TV soaps to convey messages about the benefits of physical activity. One of these storylines ran in *EastEnders*: Barry Evans' scare over his heart meant that he tried to cancel his wedding to Janine (ironically his real nemesis was Janine, rather than his health). Other obviously message-oriented storylines have included one which encouraged the older members of *EastEnders* to take up the offer of a flu jab, and a long-running one on HIV.

Frequently, following an issue-based storyline on *EastEnders*, the BBC runs a continuity message and screen graphic, giving a telephone helpline number for anyone 'affected by any of the issues featured in this storyline'. This has been used for recent storylines such as domestic violence, rape and children in care.

Theorists disagree about exactly how both explicit and more implicit messages and values work in relation to the audience. According to some theorists they have a real impact on the way that we think and act.

O'Sullivan, Dutton and Rayner state:

> Ideology is a complex concept, but broadly speaking, refers to a set of ideas which produces a partial and selective view of reality. This in turn serves the interests of those with power in society … the notion of ideology entails widely held ideas or beliefs, which may often be seen as 'common sense', legitimising or making widely acceptable certain forms of social inequality. In doing so, ideologies are able to disguise or suppress the real structure of domination and exploitation which exists in society. (1998, p72)

In contrast with this hegemonic model of how messages and values influence people, the pluralist model argues that most messages conveyed by the media are not deliberate attempts to control or influence the audience. Soaps simply reflect the views of the audience and reinforce what they already believe. Audiences choose the programmes they watch, and other media, on the basis that they fit in with their own outlook on the world. Like the uses and gratifications theory which identifies different ways in which audiences use soaps (see page 37), this model perceives audiences as active rather than 'acted upon'.

- Students could consider the idea that the soap genre presents a politically reactionary view of the world. Does the narrative present the characters as accepting their position in society and not challenging the status quo? To what extent are class and gender inequalities presented as natural and therefore perpetuated by soaps?

See **Worksheet 16 Messages and values**

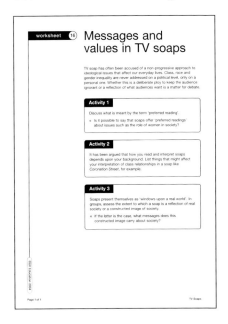

Worksheet 17 Devise and launch a new TV soap suggests a role play/simulation activity as a way of drawing together, reviewing and using everything students have learned in this course.

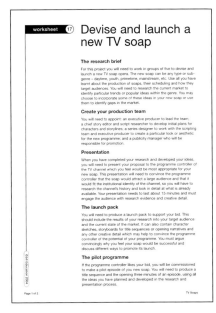
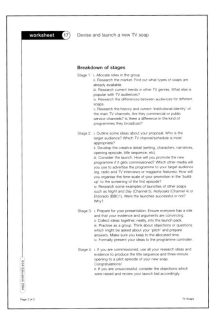

3

Case studies

The following case studies indicate how you might apply these categories, concepts and theoretical considerations to specific soaps. These examples may seem somewhat out-of-date as the storylines in soaps tend to move on very quickly, and we presume that you will develop your own up-to-date case study material for use in the classroom.

Case study 1: *EastEnders*: 'Bloody, bleak and brilliant'

> One of the most gripping, skilful and important programmes in British television history. (Andy Medhurst, The Observer, 5 February 1995)

While we might not all go as far as Andy Medhurst in his eulogy of *EastEnders*, there is no doubting the symbolic importance of the programme to the BBC in its role as public service broadcaster. Although this has not been accepted by all (there are many critics who see the programme as a result of a cynical drive for ratings and a lowering of BBC standards) for 18 years the BBC has pointed to its flagship programme as an example of its commitment to deliver quality programmes which have a broad popular appeal.

In the Christmas Day 2003 ratings *EastEnders* achieved second place with an audience of 14 million (BBC1's *Only Fools and Horses* was first). This gave BBC1 Controller Lorraine Heggessey the opportunity to make the point again:

> Providing great entertainment for all the family at Christmas is an important public service. It's great to see the audience throw open its doors to BBC faces in a range of original home-grown programmes. (The Guardian, 27 December 2003)

At a time when the BBC is under attack and its future is uncertain, the importance of EastEnders to the BBC should not be underestimated.

EastEnders

● The birth of *EastEnders*

EastEnders was first broadcast at 7pm on 19 February 1985. The original ideas came from producer Julia Smith and writer Tony Holland, an established team who had previously worked together on successful programmes such as *Z Cars*, *Angels* and *District Nurse*.

In the early 1980s, the BBC was looking for a primetime soap which could rival *Coronation Street* and *Emmerdale Farm*. ITV dominated the ratings; the BBC's early evening audience share was only around half that of ITV. Michael Grade, then Controller of BBC1, recognised the need for a successful soap to build audience loyalty.

A talk show featuring Terry Wogan was running on Monday, Wednesday and Friday and *EastEnders* was scheduled to fill the gap on the remaining days. Despite the programme being preceded by weeks of publicity and TV advertisements which introduced the characters individually, the first episode, which featured the death of Albert Square resident Reg Cox, received only lukewarm reviews. However, as the intrigue heightened over who was the father of teenager Michelle's baby and The Queen Vic's publican 'Dirty Den' was implicated, the ratings went up and up.

The interest was fuelled by tabloid coverage of the controversial storylines, illustrated by The Star's headline 'DEN DONE IT' when Den was revealed as the father. How much of this was skilfully engineered by the programme's press officer, Cheryl Ann Wilson, is hard to say. A blurring between the actors and their characters in tabloid stories reinforced the 'realism' of the programme and generated more interest: 'MY WIFE STILL LOVES ME SAYS DIRTY DEN'. (The News of The World, 6 October, 1985).

Even more debate and interest in the programme was inadvertently encouraged by Mary Whitehouse of the National Viewers' and Listeners' Association; she complained that the programme undermined family values. 'Every time [Mary Whitehouse] opens her mouth we get two million extra viewers'. (Wendy Richard, who plays Pauline Fowler, quoted in Clarke, 1987). By Christmas of the first year, *EastEnders* was reaching an audience of 22.15 million and was the most popular programme in Britain.

As David Buckingham (1987) points out, the concept of the programme was not that different from *Coronation Street*, with its setting in an enclosed working-class, inner-city community. Playing safe and keeping some aspects of the successful formula of *Coronation Street*, while changing others, such as the regionality, was no doubt another important reason for the programme's success.

- **Production**

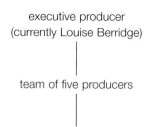

executive producer
(currently Louise Berridge)
|
team of five producers
|
production block of four episodes for each week
(produced in eight-day cycles, from Tuesday to Tuesday)

Each episode is filmed six weeks before it goes out on air. Once the programme has been recorded it is edited by the director, the videotape editor and the production assistant. This usually takes two to three days. As the programme needs to fit into the schedule exactly, the finished programme may need some last-minute editing to make sure it is exactly the correct length – 27 minutes and 15 seconds. After this a dub is done to add in any music and other sound effects needed to help construct the realism of the scenes.

- **Funding and costs**

EastEnders, like all BBC programming, is funded by the licence fee. The exact cost of making each programme varies according to whether there is any location shooting or if any special effects are needed, such as for the house fire which killed Tom and wife beater Trevor Morgan (31 October 2002).

The average cost of one hour's entertainment programming on BBC1 for the period 2002–3 was £177,300 while dramas cost £526,700 (BBC Annual Report – available on the company's website). *EastEnders*, as a primetime soap, probably falls midway between these figures. The figure for *EastEnders* given by Dorothy Hobson (2003) is £260,000 per hour; this is based on interviews she carried out in 1999, so costs are likely to have risen since then. However, soaps are highly cost-effective: *EastEnders* rarely shoots on location and works on a production-line schedule which helps to minimise costs.

● Scheduling

Originally *EastEnders* was scheduled for 7pm on Tuesdays and Thursdays, but BBC1 Controller Michael Grade strategically changed the time to 7.30pm in September 1985, to avoid clashing with the established soap *Emmerdale* on ITV. Dedicated soap viewers could catch a quality soap every day of the week in the 7.30pm slot as *Coronation Street* ran on alternate days. In April 1994 *EastEnders* began transmitting three nights a week, and in August 2001 the show began broadcasting every weekday night except Wednesday.

- Get students to discuss whether this last is a successful change or if the programme is now shown too often. How has this increase in transmission affected the programme?

This early evening slot means that the audience is maximised: most adults have arrived home from work by then and prepared the evening meal and young people and children have not yet gone to bed. *EastEnders* is usually packaged between other primetime entertainment programmes such as *Changing Rooms* (home decoration/game show) and *My Family* (sitcom). It has also been used to attract audiences to other programmes. Peter Salmon, ex-BBC1 Controller, attributes the unlikely success of *Walking with Dinosaurs* (average audiences of 13 million, the highest ever for a science programme) to its scheduling directly after *EastEnders* (so it benefited from what is known by schedulers as 'the inheritance factor').

> I think that *Dinosaurs* being that successful owes an awful lot to a brilliant run of *EastEnders*. (Quoted in Hobson, 2003)

● Marketing and press coverage

EastEnders' popularity is reinforced in a variety of ways. Many magazines and newspapers feature gossip about upcoming storylines and the actors. The tabloid press has had a close relationship with *EastEnders* from its conception, exploiting stories about the cast's criminality and relationships to boost sales. A wide range of official and unofficial merchandise, including books, calendars, computer games and knitting patterns, is available.

The BBC *EastEnders* website is another important marketing tool. Stylishly designed, it provides trivia for fans who want to be entertained and slightly more weighty information for students who want to find out about the production process. It encourages interactivity with polls such as 'Which storyline's been the most gripping?' and interpellates, or draws in, the viewer, making them feel part of a privileged group, with 'You'll laugh at these Albert Square crackers.' There are even three webcams in different locations in the square which allow fans to watch the production process. At the time of writing, the *EastEnders* website was getting between 3.5 and 4.5 million hits per week.

- **Locations**

Exterior Albert Square material is filmed outside on a custom-built set and the interior scenes are recorded at Stage One, the main studio complex at Elstree which houses the major interior sets. The Queen Victoria pub, the café and the launderette are permanent, while other sets such as the inside of individual characters' houses or upstairs at The Vic are assembled specifically for scenes as they are required. Also see Surface realism (page 55).

- **Themes**

The themes central to *EastEnders* are essentially melodramatic: they are concerned with issues that are very 'close to home'. The programme focuses on relationships – sexual and familial. Common story threads centre around problems within these: illicit sexual relationships, the discovery of familial relationships that characters did not know existed, such as Zoe's discovery that she is Kat Slater's daughter, not her sister. Other plotlines broadly fit in with the themes identified as common to TV soaps by Stewart *et al*: love, conflict, secrets, sickness, injury, skeletons in the cupboard, and plans going wrong (see page 28).

The concept of family loyalty plays an important role in providing narrative impetus. A great deal of conflict arises out of the needs of some characters to escape the bonds of the family while others try to tie them tighter. The Slaters, the Fowlers and the Mitchells are very good examples of sites for this conflict. These families rarely fit into comfortable, traditional family units, but are continually shifting, reflecting the complex nature of the contemporary family and exploring its different definitions.

- **Representations**

Class

It could be argued that *EastEnders*, in its desire to attract audiences with exciting storylines, portrays working-class people as overly violent and self-interested. Andy Medhurst critically points out that,

> The really questionable aspect of the way EastEnders utilises its setting lies in its seemingly endless love affair with gangsterism and geezerdom, its line of thug-studs that runs from Dirty Den to Grunting Grant. (The Observer, 5 February 1995)

However, the key to the programme's success with male audiences may be because this aggression leads to action rather than talk.

Brawls in The Vic are a regular feature; many of the characters, such as the Slaters and the Mitchells, are quick to argue and resort to fighting. The website encourages this representation, with a whole section of stills devoted to previous storylines which have included fights: 'Dennis lashes out' and 'Laura attacks Janine with a pan of boiling milk'. Yet other characters are thoughtful, considerate and loving at all times.

- Ask students to discuss whether this kind of violent, mud-slinging behaviour is part of *EastEnders*' charm or if it could be reduced without the programme losing its intensity.

The extended family

All of the characters in *EastEnders* are linked by a detailed and comprehensive backstory which motivates the way they interact and fuels further conflict. Many of the characters are related to one another – albeit tenuously, and this membership of a family group is often the basis for character relationships. For instance, Pat Butcher accepts a certain responsibility for Janine as she is the daughter of her ex-husband Frank.

Although new audiences may not remember Dirty Den from his first appearance in the series as the publican of The Queen Victoria, his relationship with Sharon (his adopted daughter with his wife Angie), Dennis (his illegitimate son by a mistress, Jan) and Vicki (his illegitimate daughter by Sharon's friend Michelle Fowler) and the repercussions of his former actions encourage them to accept his recent return to the programme despite the fact he has been effectively dead (falling into the canal having been shot at point blank range) for 14 years. A wonderful example of the expedient complexities of soap narratives, his return also opens up many more narrative possibilities for the scriptwriters.

The matriarch

Strong matriarchal figures are particularly evident in *EastEnders*, as they once were in *Coronation Street*. Andy Medhurst suggests that the positive nostalgia for the East End in Tony Holland's original scripts for the programme was

> the nostalgia of a gay man for a proletarian matriarchy, precisely the same sensibility that, in a Mancunian variant, had led Tony Warren to create *Coronation Street*. (The Observer, 5 February 1995)

Case studies

Lou Beale was the original matriarch of *EastEnders*; scriptwriters softened her brittle, controlling character to some extent after audiences complained about her interference in others' affairs. After Lou's death, Pauline Fowler took over as the central influential matriarch. Presently Pauline's influence seems to be waning, as she fulfils the stereotype of nagging housewife, and other matriarchal figures such as Peggy Mitchell and Mo Harris have taken over the prominent storylines. All three share similar character attributes: they need to feel they are in control of their family; this desire derives from an imperative that states that the family should be a force to be reckoned with in the local community and that its reputation should remain intact.

The character of Sharon Watts, having attended 'the school of hard knocks', plays the role of 'matriarch-in-waiting' but perhaps more in the mode of Bet Lynch from *Coronation Street* (but without the undeniably camp appeal of her outrageous make-up, earrings and dress sense). This kind of matriarch, unfettered by children and driven by a strong desire to prove her dissenters wrong, often succeeds in the man's world of business while remaining a strong ally to her female counterparts.

- Ask students to consider whether the matriarchs in *EastEnders* are positive or negative characters.

Gender

As in other soaps, the stereotypical view of society, which represents men in important roles and women as their subordinates, is challenged by *EastEnders*. As the concerns of women are centre stage, traditionally the most important space has been the home. More recently, women have been owners of two important businesses: The Vic and E2, now renamed by Sharon as Angie's Den. Pat Butcher has also always been portrayed as having a strong business sense. However, too much career success and promotion for women would take them away from the square; therefore the conventions of the genre restrict the representations of women. In his absence (having escaped from prison), Phil Mitchell's sister, Sam Mitchell, is vying with Sharon and Ian Beale for the role of *entrepreneur*.

Dot Cotton, traditionally quite a conservative character, has now married Jim Branning (Sonia's grandfather) and has made sure that he pulls his weight around the house by putting a housework rota in place. However, her power is expressed in the domestic arena and she previously worked at the launderette, a very stereotypically female role.

Men are often offered a narrower range of roles in soaps; masculine qualities that would be celebrated in other genres are often perceived as negative in the soap genre. The successful businessman, Ian Beale, is demonised; his determination and ruthlessness are not represented as positive but lead him to humiliate ex-wife Laura by ensuring she catches her lover Garry *in flagrante delicto* with his estranged wife Lynne. Nevertheless, there are strong male roles in *EastEnders*, which helps to account for the soap's popularity with male audiences. Even though Phil Mitchell is cast in the mould of the 'thug-stud', he is represented as a man who has sustained relationships, feels loyalty to his mother and children, and is able to express emotions. One of the reasons for *EastEnders*' success in the ratings on Christmas Day 2003 may be the combination of the action plot of Phil's quest for revenge and the generic 'feminised' soap elements of heightened emotionality Phil is shown to feel as he leaves the square.

Race

Until quite recently *EastEnders* failed to present any plausible black or ethnic characters; they tended to be presented in stereotypical ways. When the Tavernier family were first introduced into Albert Square in the 1990s, they were represented as Gospel-singing evangelists, a somewhat limited representation. The current representatives of different ethnic minorities, the Truman family and the Ferreiras, are, within the conventions of the soap, all multi-faceted characters with strong parts in the storylines that don't exclusively revolve around issues of race. However, the writers have also been able to directly address some issues related to colour and culture through these characters.

A virtual community

The community represented in *EastEnders* is essentially unrealistic, a nostalgic, mythologised notion that conforms to soap's generic conventions. Undoubtedly this is one of the reasons for the genre's popularity; in the absence of such a community in their own lives, audiences can experience the trials and tribulations, emotional ups and downs, and the safety and comfort of this constructed East End community.

Humour often arises from the cockney stereotypes, such as when Alfie Moon (the latest landlord of the Vic) asks the stand-in registrar for his wedding to Kat to bring a 'whistle' ('whistle and flute' is Cockney rhyming slang for 'suit'), only to find that that is exactly what he has brought. The insecurities and tensions within the community – as, for example, when Phil Mitchell reappears seeking vengeance against those who have 'done him down' – add to the drama and interest.

- Ask students to discuss whether the representations of class, gender and race in *EastEnders* are demeaning or empowering?

● Realism

Surface realism

The 'surface' realism or the verisimilitude of the *mise en scène* is authentically and carefully constructed in *EastEnders*; props, costumes and sets all work together to present a coherent and familiar world. The décor at Pat Butcher's house reflected her 'larger than life' persona (as well as her earrings), while Janine's short skirts and plunging necklines fit her promiscuous reputation. The interior of The Queen Vic is portrayed as a traditional East End pub and the café, a traditional 'greasy spoon'.

EastEnders has not resorted to extreme plotlines such as *Emmerdale*'s Lockerbie-style plane crash or *Brookside*'s siege to maintain high ratings; its avoidance of unconvincing events and concentration upon the mundane have contributed to its enduring popularity. The successful ratings suggest that audiences can identify with the emotional aspects of the soap and find the events and characters plausible. Many plotlines are close to our own experiences, but just a little exaggerated, such as Alfie Moon's last minute panic over his wedding (Christmas Day, 2003).

Classic realist style
EastEnders utilises a classic realist style in that it does not draw attention to its methods of construction. Its aim is to draw the audience in and not to challenge their preconceptions. The style is voyeuristic: the use of invisible editing techniques and convincing *mise en scène* leads us to believe we are gaining a privileged view into a real world. However, since the programme's early days there have been experiments which pushed at the boundaries of the genre – some episodes have focused on just two key characters, for example. Although some audiences may be unsettled by these apparent challenges to the generic conventions, they are quickly reassured as *EastEnders* returns to the accepted pattern of the soap genre.

Social realism
Like *Coronation Street*, *EastEnders*' style borrows heavily from the social realist tradition. Its urban setting and working-class characters are used to present a realistic picture of that world. *EastEnders* has been praised for its ability to deal with important social issues, while also being criticised for being over-didactic. Over the years the inhabitants of Albert Square have become more tolerant of HIV and homosexuality, seen the effects that drugs have upon individuals, and the consequences of teenage pregnancy. Some characters have experienced homelessness.

However, it is important to recognise that these issues are dealt with on a personal level through the characters' responses to the situations they find themselves in; no effort is made by the narrative itself to address wider issues such as why homelessness exists or women continue to suffer domestic violence. Some critics argue that soap operas such as *EastEnders* are inherently reactionary, blaming individuals for problems they have no control over, when there could be some attempt to place individuals' problems in a wider political and social context. For an interesting discussion on a similar debate, see the chapter on the 'social problem' film in John Hill's *Sex, Class and Realism* (1986).

● Ideology and audience

As mentioned, the current debate over whether violent scenes in soaps can encourage violent behaviour in children is an interesting one to investigate with students. In their annual report, published in July 2003, the Broadcasting Standards Commission voiced serious concern over 'the increase of scenes featuring intense and protracted violence' in *EastEnders* and *Coronation Street*. There had been an increasing number of complaints by viewers about soaps, particularly because they are broadcast pre-watershed. BSC research estimated that around two million children from four to 15 years old watch *EastEnders*. The research also showed that children often believed violence was an essential or inevitable way of solving a problem.

Education Secretary Charles Clarke attacked television aimed at children and programmes like soaps which sometimes ignored the watershed. Using the BSC research, he claimed a direct link between television violence and behaviour:

> The main argument which I want to challenge, about which there is too much acceptance, is that violence on television has no effect on children. I think it does ... It needs investigating ... Violence on television encourages people to grow up thinking that violence is an acceptable way of operating. (The Observer, 28 December 2003)

Clarke's view links to the hypodermic model of media effects theory. This suggests that audiences are prompted to copy the behaviour of characters on screen.

These concerns are not new. From its early days *EastEnders* has been criticised for showing events such as murder, rape and burglary, for fear that audiences would see these actions as acceptable and imitate them. This (and the swearing) formed the basis of Mary Whitehouse's long-lasting campaign against the programme. An earlier BSC report *Soap Box or Soft Soap* stated that it is a widely held view that the violence featured in soaps is too strong for children and may cause distress as well as encourage violent behaviour. The Christmas Day episode of *EastEnders* 2001 was specifically criticised by the BSC for featuring the stark image of Mo Slater hitting her violent husband over the head with an iron. There were concerns that this action implied to audiences that it is sometimes right to respond to violence with violence.

Yet other commentators argue that soaps can be a force for good:

> Nor do I see around me a sink of amorality in which our children have no moral guidance. Quite the opposite. Soap operas are almost entirely constructed out of moral fables, in which good is understood to be good and bad is almost inevitably punished. (David Aaronovitch, The Observer, 7 December 2003)

However, it must be said here that, in many cases, the punishment is a very long time coming or does not actually fit the crime. Violent characters and storylines in *EastEnders* have an undeniable cachet, especially given the interest in East End crime revived by recent films such as Guy Ritchie's *Lock, Stock and Two Smoking Barrels* (1998). As an aside, it is significant that one of the leading actors, Martin Kemp, in *The Krays* (Pete Medak, 1990), was a major character in *EastEnders* for several years. Such strong male characters, who migrate between the archetypes of villain and hero, are important to the more contemporary appeal of *EastEnders* to both sexes.

By addressing controversial issues, the programme can hopefully help make people more tolerant, for example, in the high profile given to the presentation of HIV through the popular character of Mark Fowler. The depiction of the issue in *EastEnders* can be said to have helped normalise the problem and challenge the audience's prejudices. Those who regard audiences essentially as active in their engagement with the media would argue that while *EastEnders* is not powerful in itself, it encourages people to talk and think about new ideas.

Discuss these different points of view with students:

- Do they think their behaviour has been affected by a storyline in *EastEnders*?
- Do they agree with Education Secretary Charles Clarke that there should be fewer scenes of violence in *EastEnders* or share Aaronovitch's point of view?

Case study 2: *Neighbours*: Everybody needs them?

Neighbours is a useful case study for comparison with British soaps as it features significant differences. The community of *Neighbours* is depicted as bright and positive: parents and children have primarily happy relationships, locations are colourful and sunny, and characters interact with each other cheerfully. Dorothy Hobson (2003) highlights the importance of the weather, symbolic of the optimism of the programme, and cultural differences, which are perhaps a reflection of living in a sunny climate; both these features have helped to make the soap a success. She also argues that the soap's ability to attract young audiences through its positive representations of young people was highly influential on British soaps and led to the development of *Hollyoaks* for Channel 4.

• The birth of *Neighbours*

Neighbours, a family soap set in the outskirts of Melbourne, is the longest-running, non-UK soap broadcast in this country. The original idea came from the then Head of Drama at Grundy Television, Reg Watson. He had been responsible in the past for other successful soaps such as *The Young Doctors*, *Prisoner Cell*

Block H and the British soap *Crossroads*, and wanted the main theme of this new show to be communication between parents and their children. First broadcast on Australia's Channel Seven in 1985, it proved unpopular with audiences and was axed after 170 episodes. In 1986, Ten Network took over the programme and gave it a new lease of life, writing out some of the older characters and introducing several teenage actors, including Jason Donovan and Kylie Minogue. They also made the show more upmarket, and spent a great deal of money promoting it in Sydney, traditionally a rival city to Melbourne, by sending the cast to meet the public and make personal appearances. Seventeen years later, *Neighbours* is viewed in over 60 countries by more than 120 million viewers every day, providing a lucrative income for Grundy.

- **Production**

The exteriors for *Neighbours* are filmed at Pin Oak Court on the outskirts of Melbourne. The street was chosen because of its proximity to the studios where the indoor shots would be filmed and also because it was fairly isolated and easily accessible from the back, allowing large production vehicles to be parked out of range of the cameras. This location is used by the production crew two or three times a week, but most of the filming happens at the studios.

Neighbours

A production team of approximately 60 people work on the five episodes that are filmed every week for 48 weeks of the year. Overall, it takes 12 weeks to complete each block of five episodes from start to finish. This includes scriptwriting, research, filming and editing. A pool of 12 writers generates ideas and meets regularly with production staff to agree how the storylines should progress. Grundy sells *Neighbours* to Ten Network which operates as a commercial station, raising its finances through the sale of advertising.

● Scheduling

Despite being screened before the evening primetime slot, *Neighbours* soon won an audience of five million in Australia. Its success was noticed by BBC1 Controller Michael Grade, who bought the programme to enliven the BBC's daytime schedule in 1986. Initially it was screened twice a day: at 9.05am and at lunchtime. Many people liked the programme but found the scheduling slots impossible to catch. Nevertheless, *Neighbours* developed a huge following in this country with an audience ranging from students to pensioners. Michael Grade noted that his daughter Alison and her friends watched the show during the holidays and rescheduled it to the teatime slot at 5.35pm, immediately after children's television in order to gain young viewers during term time. The audience grew to 16 million at its peak in the late 1980s, even beating *EastEnders* and *Coronation Street*. While recent audience figures are nearer the four million mark, *Neighbours* maintains a steady audience and fan base.

● Marketing and press coverage

Like other popular soaps, *Neighbours* is supported by an official website, providing information and gossip about plotlines and stars. The bright, primary colours and design of the website can be compared with the darker, more serious mode of address of the *EastEnders* site; the *Neighbours* site seems predominantly aimed at youngsters. Students should also check out www.perfectblend.net as it contains useful background, interviews and storyboards of the title sequence.

No specialist magazines about *Neighbours* are published in Australia but UK magazines such as Inside Soap and teen magazines such as TV Hits often feature its stars. Generally, they do not make headlines as frequently as UK soap stars do in the UK tabloid press, but current and past *Neighbours'* stars do so when appearing in other guises, for example in the pop world. Kylie Minogue has gone on to become Australia's highest earning woman, while Holly Valance is featured regularly in pop magazines and the UK tabloid press because of her success in the British charts.

- **Locations**

Neighbours depends upon two or three main settings. The central setting is Ramsay Street (Pin Oak Court). This location includes five homes, two of which belong to Lou Carpenter (one currently rented by Libby Kennedy, and the other by Toadie, Dee and Stuart); the other houses are occupied by the Scullys, Harold and recent arrivals, the Hoylands. Very little action actually takes place in the road outside the houses, but establishing shots of them make it clear to the audience which family is the focus of each narrative strand. Very close to Ramsay Street (or so we assume, as the characters seem to spend a great deal of their leisure time there) is a small complex, comprising a hotel and Harold's coffee shop; set in a park, it allows for more narrative opportunities. Occasionally, the story visits Erinsborough High School.

All these locations are brightly lit and convey a sense of well-being. The characters seem to enjoy a lot of leisure time in which to hang out together, and this is perhaps one of the pleasures for the audience.

- **Use of music**

The lack of social realism that pervades *Neighbours* is reflected in its use of music. Unlike British soaps, non-diegetic music is used to comment on scenes and elevate their emotional impact, as well as to mark a change of scene.

Neighbours' Music Director Chris Pettifer states:

> Sometimes it is better to make it so you don't actually notice the music and drift in and out of the dialogue. Other times, when we feel the scene hasn't gone as intended, we use the music to deliberately drag the audience by their ears to the feeling we want for the moment. So sometimes subtle and other times sledgehammer! (www.perfectblend.net)

- **Themes**

Despite covering many of the main topics central to soap, *Neighbours* rarely focuses on anything controversial. It is not a social realist text in the mould of *Coronation Street* or *EastEnders*. While Reg Watson's original ideas for the programme centred on problems within family relationships, these issues rarely cause serious ructions between the characters. Relationships between parents and children and neighbours are represented more positively. The Scullys are used to explore in detail the problems that arise out of the generational divide and the conflicts between parents and their teenage children. Other storylines have demonstrated the father/son relationship as the site of ideological conflict, such as with Harold Bishop and his son David at odds over fee-paying schools and music lessons for granddaughter Serena.

However, while young people's interests and concerns are dealt with, they are not usually represented as serious problems. Although Dorothy Hobson (2003) regards this as 'more natural and realistic' than any other soap opera at the time when *Neighbours* began, critics have argued that it promotes a false ideology of 'happy families' – a comfortably constructed artifice. Consequently, the soap may lack emotional realism or depth.

As a teatime show it has to be appropriate for a family audience, so *Neighbours* does not attempt to address some of the issues that have been aired in British soaps: domestic violence, murder and crime. The characters experience little, if any, poverty or hardship and consequently a key narrative strand of many soap operas, which involves women struggling on their own to retain their dignity and their standing in the community, cannot be explored.

Although *EastEnders*' characters explore political issues such as homelessness and unemployment only on a personal level, the topics are at least brought to the attention of the audience. In avoiding major conflict, *Neighbours* reflects a kind of middle of the road, or consensus, Australian vision which does not set out to rock any social or political boats. None of its characters are black or working class and so none of the issues that affect those groups are written into the narrative. It could be argued that this reflects ideological attitudes that prevail in Australia.

● Representations

Class

Dorothy Hobson argues that representations of class in *Neighbours* are different from British soaps because Australia is 'a society without a clear definition of class' (2003). The characters are basically middle class, with work roles that include a doctor, a nurse, a headmistress, a publican and landlord, a café owner, a hotel owner, a vicar and a solicitor. Other characters have manual jobs: Joe Scully is a builder, and the recently demised Drew was a mechanic. However, both men own or owned their own businesses and employ other people. There are few really working-class characters; Joe Scully's family are alone in representing working-class traits: Steph Scully works for a car parts delivery company and her sister is a receptionist at the local hotel.

The picture of Australian life presented to its international audience is one of harmony and wealth. The show perpetuates a stereotypical image of Australians as basically good-natured and easy-going, living in a world of little social or political disruption. Nobody is poor or has to struggle for a living. This is one of its greatest attractions for audiences who want to lose themselves in a fantasy after a hard day at work or at school.

Gender
Gender representations in *Neighbours* are on the whole positive. Most of the women have careers and lead independent and interesting lives. Unlike its British counterparts, it does not rely on the same stock female soap stereotypes. Even older women are represented in positive terms: Helen Daniels, a woman in her sixties, had a number of romances and a successful career, as well as offering stability to her family. While the role of 'gossip' was filled by Mrs Mangel and the 'nagging housewife' by Madge Bishop, there have been no matriarchs like Elsie Tanner or Pauline Fowler. The older women may be respected for their wisdom, but do not rule over an extended family and are not forces to be reckoned with. There have also been a number of positive representations of single fathers bringing up their families, such as Jim Robinson.

Race
As previously mentioned, there are virtually no ethnic characters in *Neighbours* although the other Australian, daytime soap, *Home and Away*, regularly features Greek characters.

A cosy community
Essentially, *Neighbours* glosses over issues which are uncomfortable for the white Australian audience to deal with. Representations of race are notable by their absence: in its 17 years' run there has only been one aboriginal character and one black character. Issues relating to the new immigrant populations are never touched upon.

As with most soaps, the characters are associated through their joint histories and experiences and although *Neighbours* does not feature the powerful family dynasties that other programmes do, the characters are linked through friendship and loyalty to one another. The nuclear family unit predominates and single parents (except for widowed single parents) or divorced families rarely feature.

Occasionally a story does deal with difficult circumstances which cause friction. In a plotline of 2002, for example, Susan Kennedy lost her memory as a result of a blow to the head. The accident left her unable to remember anything past her 16th birthday, and subsequently she has struggled to deal with the established adult relationships important to her before the incident. Previously a headmistress and perfect mother/wife figure, Susan initially absolves herself from all responsibilities and goes back to university, although she does return to her job later on. The arising conflict mainly centred on her inability to relate to her husband and her children.

Homelessness among the young has been featured as an issue; Harold (and, in the past, Madge, his late wife) has taken in a variety of boys in need of a good upbringing and clear moral guidance. Harold's association with the church and his high standing in the community make him an ideal candidate for this role and with him as their patron, the boys usually become responsible and functioning members of society again. In this way problems are contained and resolved, but the darker, less desirable side of community life remains hidden.

- **The pleasures of *Neighbours***

Mark Little, who played Joe Mangel, has said

> We don't talk to our own neighbours, but we watch neighbours on telly talking. (The Soap Opera: Fiction or Reality, BBC2, 1999)

This is one of the key pleasures in watching TV soap, probably particularly so for *Neighbours* with its rosy outlook on life.

The programme has often been criticised for its suburban and uncontroversial view of Australian society, but this may be at the root of its popularity. Audiences engage with *Neighbours* very differently to the way they engage with British soaps like *EastEnders* and *Coronation Street*. *Neighbours* is aimed at a wide audience, allowing all members of the family to view it together. Its scheduling slot means that for a large number of people it provides a way of unwinding after a day at work: the show fulfils the role of a relaxant.

A friend and fellow teacher described her experience of being a regular *Neighbours* viewer as not unlike getting into a warm bath every evening. The lack of controversial storylines and the non-radical viewpoints mean that the audience is rarely challenged and the gratifications it provides reflect this.

- Ask students to consider to what extent *Neighbours* would have to change if it were rescheduled in a primetime slot.

Case study 3: Coronation Street: Paradise on Earth

> At half-past seven tonight I shall be in paradise. (John Betjeman on *Coronation Street*, quoted by Watson and Hill, 1999)

- **The birth of *Coronation Street***

Britain's longest-running TV soap *Coronation Street* was first broadcast on 9 December 1960. Made by Granada Television, an independent TV company based in Manchester, episodes were originally recorded live and shown twice a week. The programme's strong regional and working-class identity has been essential from the outset and the programme's creator/writer, Tony Warren, was keen to base the serial in the north of England:

Coronation Street

> 'Three months ago I decided to write a serial about the north. I started with one household, it became two, then three, and then a whole street, and I had to add a pub, an off-licence and a place of worship … What I have aimed at is a true picture of life [in the north] and the people's basic friendliness and essential humour. (TV Times, 4–10 December 1960)

As mentioned above, this was consistent with the trend for 'kitchen sink' or social realist dramas, which became popular in British film and television during the late 1950s and throughout the 1960s. Films such as: *Billy Liar* (John Schlesinger, 1963), *Saturday Night and Sunday Morning* (Karel Reisz, 1960), *The L-Shaped Room* (Bryan Forbes, 1962) and *This Sporting Life* (Lindsay Anderson, 1963) aimed to show realistic depictions of working-class life which challenged former commonplace stereotypical representations and explored lives of ordinary people in greater detail.

Despite critics of the time dismissing the 'domestic drudgery' of *Coronation Street*, the programme was an instant popular success with audiences. After a pilot run of 13 episodes, shown in the north west of England, it was screened nationally on the ITV network from May 1961. The programme's ratings remained unrivalled on British television for over 20 years, and it consistently topped viewing charts, with audiences of between 13 and 19 million for each episode. It was not until the BBC launched *EastEnders*, its own working-class soap, in 1985 that *Coronation Street* had any significant competition from British television soaps for its audience.

- It is worth looking at some of the books that have been written about *Coronation Street*, including academic studies and memoirs of stars. A number of TV programmes, such as a *The South Bank Show* special and 25th anniversary retrospective, are available commercially or from public libraries.
- If you have not watched the programme yourself, it is illuminating to talk to long-standing fans to gain their perspective on how the programme has developed. Students could interview friends and family about it.

● **Production**

- Granada TV produces a pack for teachers, which gives a detailed breakdown of their production schedule and an overview of the programme's history.

There are about 15 writers working for the programme at any one time, whose work is supported and overseen by the story editor, three storyline writers, and a programme historian, whose job it is to keep a detailed archive on all the characters and previous storylines to ensure continuity. Each writer usually works on one episode at a time and has about a week to complete a final version. The producer chairs a script conference every two weeks to discuss possible script ideas and allocate developmental writing responsibilities. Storyline writers produce synopses of the basic ideas, which will be developed by the writers into specific episodes. The ideas discussed at this meeting are usually being planned for transmission in about three months.

The filming and production schedule on *Coronation Street* is strictly controlled and works on a rolling four-week cycle for each weekly series of episodes. The producer and script department liaise with four directors, each working on one week's set of episodes at a time. While one director collects his/her scripts and begins initial preparations for filming, a second director will be in their second week of preparations and rehearsal; a third director will actually be recording their week's episodes and a fourth director will be completing final editing of the episodes for transmission that week.

In the first week of the production cycle, the director identifies the design, casting and location requirements and liaises with the relevant departments to organise the detail. The initial script must also be transcribed into a camera script. This is a detailed visual interpretation of each scene and identifies camera shots, as well as the precise positioning of actors within the scene (blocking). During rehearsals, blocking is essential to enable technical staff to co-ordinate the camera and sound equipment with the on-screen action.

During the filming week, any location shooting which takes place away from Granada's own *Coronation Street* set is scheduled for Sunday. Outside scenes, which are shot on the street itself, take place on Monday. Recording of the remaining scenes takes place inside the studio usually on Thursday and Friday. A day's filming lasts between 8am and 7pm though can sometimes be longer.

The director plans the filming schedule in advance to make the most efficient use of the studio sets and time available. Scenes are therefore shot out of narrative sequence and require editing before transmission. The director and the production assistant usually have only eight and a half hours in which to edit the programmes. They must make sure that each episode conforms to an exact timing, in order to fit the transmission schedule and commercial breaks.

- It is quite useful to explain this kind of material visually – perhaps by drawing out a week-to-week or day-to-day diary. You can then list all the things which need to happen in each week and get students to fill in a draft schedule.

• Locations

The producers of *Coronation Street* are keen to define the programme as 'a community-based drama serial'. The settings reflect this intention, with the action taking place in or around the street, either in domestic settings, like front rooms or kitchens, or in public domains, like the shop, the factory or The Rovers Return pub. Location filming is expensive and it breaks the close, intimate community feel of the programme. As a result, it is rare.

Occasionally, a new set is needed and the designer has about four weeks to develop and buy for a new studio set. However, because filming is an ongoing process, the set must then be built in the studio when no filming is taking place. Since the only time it is not being used is at night, much set-building takes place then. This is another reason why the sets are designed for long-term use and become so familiar to viewers.

- Ask students to list all the key sets and locations in *Coronation Street*, describing them in detail. They can then compare them with the sets of another soap (for example, *EastEnders* or *Hollyoaks*) and discuss reasons behind the similarities or differences.

• Funding and costs

Granada TV uses a production line for economic efficiency. Filming rarely occurs away from the set and costs are kept low by maximising the use of in-house sets and resources. As part of ITV, the funding of *Coronation Street* has always been generated by the sale of commercial airtime within the programme: the three-minute commercial break. Because of the consistently high audience ratings, commercial airtime in *Coronation Street* is expensive, since it is the most sought after by companies hoping to reach a wide audience.

Carlton Television's media sales website recently quoted figures of between £12,000 and £49,000 for a 30-second, primetime evening slot in London. These figures specifically excluded airtime during *Coronation Street*, which suggests that the advertising rates for *Coronation Street* can exceed £50,000.

Since September 1996, *Coronation Street* has been sponsored by Cadbury Ltd. According to Granada TV's own figures, the initial partnership was worth £10 million and was unique in British television history. The sponsorship deal demonstrated the wider commercial potential of *Coronation Street* as a promotional brand and despite some challenges from other companies eager to take over the contract, Cadbury's have managed to continue this lucrative liaison. This model has now been adopted more widely in commercial television, particularly in soap, where there is a guaranteed, loyal and well-established audience.

- **Scheduling**

Coronation Street was first transmitted at 7pm on Mondays and Fridays; from May 1961 this schedule was changed to Mondays and Wednesdays. The twice-weekly schedule remained until October 1989 when a third episode was added on Fridays, partly in response to competition from the BBC (and *EastEnders* in particular) which had been building its audience share throughout the late 1980s and had, from the outset, included a third weekly show, albeit an 'omnibus' edition of the other two episodes. In November 1996 a fourth episode was added on Sundays, partly as a result of the success of daily soaps like *Neighbours*, which had proved that the audience of a soap could be sustained with a more frequent schedule.

Coronation Street has always been transmitted in the peak-time evening slot, with only minor alterations to its original 7pm time: the current Wednesday, Friday and Sunday episodes are all transmitted at 7.30pm with the Monday episode going out at 8.30pm. As mentioned above, digital and satellite TV channels are increasingly offering fans a second chance to view the evening's episode. ITV2 screens a later repeat of the day's episode of *Coronation Street* at around 10pm. (BBC3 does the same for *EastEnders*.)

- Ask fans of the soap to talk about how often they miss an episode and the strategies they use to catch up. Do they check the website, read TV guides or magazines or chat to friends who have watched it?

- **Marketing and press coverage**

In the UK, stories about *Coronation Street*'s plotlines and its stars regularly appear in the tabloid newspapers as well as in other celebrity lifestyle magazines like Hello or OK! These feature articles and photoshoots on the actors' lives, which increase fans' knowledge of and sense of intimacy with the soap's characters.

- Students are often well informed about celebrity gossip. Get them to bring in copies of recent *Coronation Street* stories from the tabloids and popular magazines and compare links between the stories and the target audience of each of the different publications. What does this suggest about the role of the *Coronation Street* press office?

Coronation Street is regularly advertised in other daytime TV magazine shows like *This Morning* and on evening chat shows like *The Frank Skinner Show*. The *Coronation Street* press office ensures that actors who are involved in particularly prominent storylines are invited onto a variety of programmes to talk about themselves, the soap and the issues raised by the storyline. This also happens on radio, particularly talk-based stations, where interviews are regularly conducted with soap stars.

- Get students to track the promotion of a particular big storyline. Check the website for details of official press releases and then look out for radio, TV and tabloid interviews.

Corrie – the brand

- A quick way to get students to realise the extent of the *Coronation Street* brand is to get students to look out for *Coronation Street* items of merchandising, particularly around Christmas. Throughout the year, card and gift shops often stock themed *Coronation Street* cards, key rings and mugs.

The sheer size and well-documented loyalty of the regular *Coronation Street* audience makes it an appealing and potentially lucrative niche market for media companies. *Coronation Street* has become a successful brand, which allows the merchandising of a panoply of items, from Rovers Return mugs and bar mats to *Coronation Street* board games. There is an official *Coronation Street* magazine and fan club and Granada TV organises special *Coronation Street* backstage tours around their Manchester studios. In common with other soaps, an official website keeps fans updated on behind-the-scenes gossip and provides detailed programme information. Granada TV also markets *Coronation Street* into territories around the world, generating further fans and revenue.

- Encourage students to investigate the *Coronation Street* website and notice the mode of address adopted. From looking at the website, how do you think Granada TV views the fans?
- What links and tie-ins are available through the website? How is ITV using *Coronation Street* to promote other products?

There is also a range of unofficial websites and chat rooms, designed by the fans themselves, which demonstrate how the programme extends the notion of community beyond traditional localised, geographical definitions. There is now an online *Coronation Street* community where fans from around the globe can access and exchange information about their favourite TV programme.

- Compare the official *Coronation Street* website with a few unofficial fan sites. What idea of the fans do you get from these sites? Is it the same as the official website profile?

● Themes

The distinctive opening title sequence of terraced rooftops and cobbled streets, together with the memorable theme tune, have remained virtually unchanged since the programme's inception in 1960. This title sequence is indicative of the central, defining theme for *Coronation Street*: the depiction of a northern, working-class community with a strong regional identity.

- Ask students to analyse the title sequence and opening shots in detail with the class, and to compare it to the opening sequence of *EastEnders*, *Hollyoaks* or *Neighbours*. What does each title sequence represent about the programme's identity?

The first ever episode used the well-established narrative technique of introducing a new character, Florrie Lindley, into *The Street*'s community. This highlighted the tight-knit nature of Weatherfield's inhabitants, foregrounding its resistance to newcomers while simultaneously demonstrating a propensity for gossip, as the established members of the community discussed the new arrival. Such features – community, gossip, regional identity – are all staple defining conventions for the soap genre. *Coronation Street* still maintains its strong regional identity and working-class theme: some scenes take place in the textiles factory, an industry associated with the north west of England and its tough working conditions.

As with other soaps, the basis of the drama revolves around families, many of whom have a long and detailed history and some members of whom, like Ken Barlow, have been featured from the start of the programme. There is a broad cross-section of generational issues, and emotional relationships are foregrounded strongly.

● Narrative

Coronation Street's narrative structure largely conforms to typical patterns of soap opera. Each episode lasts about 24 minutes in total, which allows for a commercial break during the programme and the sponsor's advertisements before and after. The structure of an episode is strictly controlled. The most essential element is the cliff-hanger (or tag) for the main storyline, which always ends the programme in order to secure the audience for the next episode. There are usually at least two other storylines running through any one episode and each of these is likely to be tagged during the programme.

It has been argued that the narrative pattern of *Coronation Street* is more evenly and 'theatrically' balanced than in other British TV soaps. If a serious or dramatic story is being covered, this is likely to be balanced by a deliberately comic storyline to ensure that the programme does not become too bleak. Some people have criticised *Coronation Street* for this policy, but Bill Podmore, a successful ex-producer of the programme, has suggested that the show should be viewed as light entertainment and should never allow conflict or controversy to dominate. As such, a typical narrative structure in a *Coronation Street* episode combines a romantic or emotional storyline with a more dramatic or tense issue and intersperses this with some comic dialogue from characters not otherwise involved in either of the stories.

Occasionally a serious or dramatic issue is allowed to dominate an episode (or series of episodes) entirely, usually when it is reaching its climax; the storyline involving a serial killer is a recent example. Often tabloid and other media coverage (engineered by the programme's press officer) support such episodes to increase the sense of drama and entice new viewers. Although *Coronation Street* does not define itself as 'issue-driven', there have been occasions, such as the imprisonment of Tricia through her problems with debt, when storylines have led to debates in Parliament.

Coronation Street draws heavily on the comedy of everyday life, as much as the tragedy. Characters such as Curly Watts (a perennially hapless clown) and Vera Duckworth (almost a pantomime dame) have become ingrained in the popular imagination as lovable fools and grotesques. This has led some commentators to dismiss its realism and suggest that it has become a parody of northern, working-class life; nevertheless, its producers claim to represent the full diversity of life and defend the quality of the writing.

- Ask students to identify the storylines in a current episode of *Coronation Street* and decide whether the show can be classed as 'light entertainment'. How does it compare with other soaps (eg *EastEnders*, *Hollyoaks* or *Neighbours*)?

● Social realism

As previously mentioned, the style of *Coronation Street* was strongly influenced by social realist film trends in the 1950s and 60s. From the outset, Tony Warren, the programme's creator, aimed to present a true picture of working-class life in the north of England, which did not romanticise or patronise its subjects. However, for the first few years of production, it was recorded live in a studio without editing, and this has also lent it a theatrical style, which relied on good character performances and high quality scripts. Despite more modern production techniques, many people consider *Coronation Street* to have retained these aesthetic values. Much of the action takes place in recognisable studio sets (the pub, the street, the factory, the home) and certain characters tend to dominate.

Despite being criticised for presenting an overly nostalgic or old-fashioned view of working-class life in the north of England, *Coronation Street* has reflected social changes and shifts over time. In the late 1960s, student protests and marches were reflected in at least one storyline, while in the late 1970s there was industrial unrest in Mike Baldwin's factory. Although the makers of *Coronation Street* claim not to follow social trends or to be involved in issue-based politics, these historical examples demonstrate the way in which social context inevitably influences storylines.

● Characters

Coronation Street has always used a stock of soap opera characters who fall into a range of archetypal roles: Peter Barlow (a 'Jack the lad'), Bet Lynch/Gilroy (the strong woman), Karen and Steve McDonald (initially at least, the 'happy' young couple), Albert Tatlock (the troublesome old boy). Nevertheless, these characters provide a sufficient point of identification for audiences to connect with their everyday experiences and identify with the 'ordinariness' of their lives, or function purely as escapist entertainment.

As with other soaps, *Coronation Street* revolves around key families to allow a broad range of stories and to aid cross-generational audience identification. Many of *The Street*'s former and current characters have become household names, even with people who do not ordinarily view the soap: Hilda Ogden, Jack and Vera Duckworth, Elsie Tanner, Bet Lynch or Mavis Riley, to name a few. This popular knowledge of the soap's key characters suggests the power the programme has to enter into people's everyday experiences and reinforce a sense of shared community, or at least, shared cultural references (see 'surveillance' in uses and gratifications theory – page 37). In this way, *Coronation Street*, its characters and the values it represents have become an essential part of British popular culture.

The Street occasionally overhauls its characters and in the past few years it has brought in younger people in response to criticisms that its format was too old-fashioned and nostalgic, appealing to older viewers but failing to attract a new generation. During the late 1990s, other soaps, like *Emmerdale*, similarly updated their format to attract a younger audience. Recently, *Coronation Street* engaged Keith Duffy, who had originally made his name in the pop world with the band Boyzone, in a further attempt to attract new viewers. When a new character is written into the show, the actor is often only given a brief outline, rather than a detailed biography. This is because the producers of *Coronation Street* like the character to evolve naturally with the storylines. This also allows the actor playing the role to develop and mould the character into someone they feel comfortable playing.

The audience for *Coronation Street* is large, with current figures around 13 million for each episode. However, audience analysis indicates that *Coronation Street* viewers are spread unevenly across geography, social class, racial and generational divides. In the early 1990s audience research showed that *EastEnders* was attracting more of the 16- to 34-year-old audience and *Coronation Street* was watched by an older, more northern viewership. Gradually, *Coronation Street* has overhauled its characters and storylines to target a younger audience.

Coronation Street is well known for its loyal gay audience and over the years, its rolling cast of *femmes fatales* and strong women and has offered ample opportunities for hosts of drag queens to lovingly recreate favourite characters (such as Rita and Bet) in pub and club performances all over the country. The trials and tribulations of key female characters at the hands of a whole procession of heterosexual male 'users and losers', have found many loyal followers.

The producers and actors of *Coronation Street* are well aware of this audience. A double-coding is evident in its occasional celebration of camp, seen in some of the more theatrical costumes, hair and make-up styles of certain characters, as well as in the use of *double entendres* and cheeky references for an informed audience. The writings and reviews of Andy Medhurst on this topic are an entertaining and informative insight.

- Ask students to watch an episode of *Coronation Street* and count the number of characters under the age of 30. Compare this with other soaps. To what extent does *Coronation Street* now have an appeal for younger audiences? What would happen if *Coronation Street* became dominated by characters under the age of 30?

Representations

Some critics have argued that the daily lives represented in Weatherfield do not reflect the actual daily lives of a northern, working-class community. However, other critics have argued that it shows recognisable elements of real life; for example, the domestic family scenes in the kitchen are likely to reflect one part of many people's everyday reality. The second view seems more reasonable, as the programme does not claim to be a documentary, but a drama based on the lives and stories of ordinary people, with the requisite heightening of events and emotions for dramatic effect.

It is also asserted that, like other soaps, *Coronation Street* provides us with real-life characters, with which to identify. This is a rather narrow and outdated view of audience response to fiction and, as stated elsewhere, it does not begin to explain the popularity of soaps with a highly diverse audience. Identification is only one of many ways in which we connect with drama; voyeurism, escapism and *Schadenfreude* are others.

● Class

Coronation Street has always had a strongly working-class profile both in terms of its audience and its characters. Tony Warren said that he deliberately set *Coronation Street* in a working-class street in the north of England because it created the potential for exploring new dramatic possibilities. By including a factory on the set, traditional class issues of employment, industrial relations and workers' rights can be covered in storylines. Before *Coronation Street* came to our screens, British television had generally represented a middle-class view of the world.

The working-class orientation of *Coronation Street* is reflected in its title sequence, which combines a distinctive, mournful theme tune, reminiscent of traditional workers' brass band music, with iconic images of terraced houses and cobbled streets. Such images have come to signify a resolutely working-class region in the popular imagination.

Nowadays, with the erosion of traditional working-class industries in the north, as well as the general blurring of class boundaries in Britain as a whole, *Coronation Street* features a mixture of lower middle-class and working-class families. Nevertheless, the factory and The Rovers Return both remain as classic signifiers of British working-class life and there has been little other 'gentrification' of *The Street*. A recent storyline concerns Karen McDonald 'crossing the line' in the factory and being promoted to supervisor. This generates conflict between her and her previous workmates, who feel she has betrayed them by 'joining the enemy'. A traditional view of employer/employee relationships thus continues to be propounded.

- Ask students to interview people aged over 50 about their view of *Coronation Street*. How do students' perceptions compare? Do the interviewees think that *Coronation Street* has changed at all in the way it represents people? Is it still working class or more classless?

● Gender

Coronation Street is renowned for its portrayal of strong female characters. In its early days, the series centred on a number of women with outgoing, forceful personalities – independent and assertive women at the heart of the community. These women have become legendary: Elsie Tanner and Ena Sharples were engaged in constant feuds and conflicts. More recently characters like Vera Duckworth, Bet Lynch and Audrey Roberts continued this tradition.

Younger female characters provide strong role models: Karen McDonald, the new factory supervisor, and Lucy Richards, who rejected Peter Barlow's marriage proposal despite facing the prospect of becoming a single mum.

- Using extracts from recent episodes, students could look at the narrative trajectory of particular female characters as well as their physical appearance, home/work environment and how it is conveyed through *mise en scène*, as well as dialogue and interaction with other characters, in analysing representation.
- They could also try to divide the different female characters into types and look at different audience responses, including their own, to these characters and how they are represented.

● Race

Despite being set in the north west of England, which has a strong multicultural profile, it took *Coronation Street* until 1995 to feature a major black or Asian character. The largely white casting policy has continued and currently there are only two or three significant Asian characters, Sunita, Dev and his new girlfriend.

As such, it is difficult to agree entirely with Roy Hattersley's claim that the soap

> now reflects the complicated class and racial structure that characterises British society. (TV Quick review, 1990, cited in McQueen, p36, 1998)

- Ask students to compare an episode of *Coronation Street* with an episode of *EastEnders* for their respective representations of race. They could use a content analysis technique over a two-week period, for example, to count the frequency of appearances by characters of colour. Or they could focus on storylines, in order to determine whether the race or ethnic origin of a character determines that storyline or, whether the narrative reflects a more fully-rounded interest in all aspects of such characters' lives.
- Students could also undertake research with a diverse audience in order to get different opinions on the representations of race in current soaps.

● *Corrie*'s community

The notion of community is fundamental to *Coronation Street*. As with other soaps there is a strong sense of family loyalty, and many of the family names have long associations with *The Street*: the Duckworths, Barlows and Battersbys.

Despite regular conflicts between the strong characters, there is nevertheless a sense of mutual support and shared values. The community represented in *Coronation Street* has been criticised for its nostalgic nature and some have suggested that the basic representation of Weatherfield community values has altered little since 1960.

This is chiefly because, in performance terms, *Coronation Street* is character-led rather than issue-based, as mentioned above. It is watched for the pure enjoyment of the theatricality of some of the performances, its colourful dialogue and tragicomic byplay between familiar characters. The actors deliver strong ensemble performances and so constitute a community in themselves; whether or not they relate to any real or notional one is largely irrelevant now, as they function as members of a virtual community, which we can eavesdrop on.

Concessions to the 21st century are arguably tokenist in *Coronation Street* and it only occasionally deals with issues related to underage sex, homosexuality and drug abuse. Even a recent storyline, which involved a transsexual and her husband paying for an illegitimate baby (Tracey Barlow's) seemed incongruous and unconvincing (except to die-hard fans, no doubt) except in melodramatic terms. Its community values are indeed very basic and nostalgic ones, based on the circulation of secrets, gossip and envy of one's neighbours!

- Ask students whether they think *Coronation Street* is a recognisable community?
- How would they dramatise their own community? Does it have anything in common with any of the TV soaps?

Case study 4: Low fat soap: *Hollyoaks*

> Long on gossip but short on blood and guts. (Radio Times, 21–7 October 1995)

Hollyoaks makes an interesting case study as students are likely to be familiar with it and can make comparisons with *EastEnders*, *Coronation Street* and *Neighbours*.

● The birth of *Hollyoaks*

The first episode of *Hollyoaks* was broadcast on Channel 4 on 23 October 1995 at 6.30pm, targeting 16- to 24-year-olds. It was originally devised to be transmitted as one 30-minute episode per week and marketed as a comedy-drama: 'funny and glamorous' (ibid). *Hollyoaks* quickly established a loyal following among its target market and Mersey Television increased production to two episodes per week.

The series was created by Phil Redmond, whose previous television successes included BBC's *Grange Hill* and Channel 4's long-running soap opera, *Brookside* (1982–2003). However, the concept of the programme was very different from the grit of *Brookside* or even the serious issues of bullying, breakdown and break-up of *Grange Hill*. When Channel 4 gave the go-ahead for two episodes per week Redmond introduced more controversial issues.

Hollyoaks

A Liverpudlian himself, Redmond was keen to establish a British soap opera set in the north of England which focused on the lives of teenagers and young people, so the programme is set in the fictional borough of Hollyoaks, somewhere close to the historic Roman city of Chester. Much of the action originally took place around a college, and, although this has widened considerably, the college is still central to the drama (the official website is presented like a college's official website – which also clearly indicates the target audience for the soap).

Despite its early evening schedule and often 'light-hearted' approach, the soap has developed a reputation for its willingness to deal with controversial issues which affect young people, like teenage pregnancy, drug abuse, male rape and self-harm. This policy has proved very successful, leading to occasional late-night episodes and the production of special 'feature-length' videos. In 1999, the series was increased to three half-hour episodes per week, increasing to four episodes in 2001. *Hollyoaks* has now become a daily soap (five episodes per week) as a result of the rescheduling and eventual axing of *Brookside*. In 2001, *Hollyoaks* was nominated for a BAFTA for 'Best Soap'.

- ## Production

The production of *Hollyoaks* is similar to the other case study soaps in this pack with a busy 'rolling' production schedule needed to keep pace with the frequency of the broadcasts.

The producer works closely with the script department to plan storylines about three months before screening. Scripts undergo several drafts and can involve more than one writer. Script editors therefore oversee the writing process and are responsible for script development, working closely with the writers to produce scripts which conform to the *Hollyoaks* 'style' and are attractive to *Hollyoaks* target audience. Script assistants liaise with the production and writing teams. They have input from storyline stage through to the final shooting script. Once the scripts are complete, the week's episodes go into production.

A production manager administers and organises the cast, crews, equipment and facilities. As with other soaps, *Hollyoaks* has a number of 'shoots' and 'crews' operating at any one time, each managing a particular set of episodes. This complicated production schedule therefore requires considerable organisation and day-to-day management. The production management team has overall responsibility for the scheduling of the various shoots, rostering staff and allocating resources appropriately.

- It is worth consulting the official *Hollyoaks*/Mersey TV websites which sometimes have job advertisements. These demonstrate the demands of working in the industry and show students the kind of qualifications and qualities that may be required.

Hollyoaks is made by Mersey Television, Phil Redmond's production company which was also responsible for *Brookside*. Both soaps have been technically innovative. (Redmond has responded to Channel 4's dropping *Brookside* by announcing plans to continue it as a DVD-only soap.) Unlike *Coronation Street*, which uses multiple cameras for each scene, *Hollyoaks* (and *Brookside* before it) uses a single camera technique in the studio. *Hollyoaks* was also the first drama series to start shooting in full widescreen using Digibeta cameras.

- Students could compare the camerawork in *Hollyoaks* and *Coronation Street*. They should identify any techniques that are different to other soaps, and discuss what the overall effect is on the visual aesthetics of each production.

• Funding and costs

Hollyoaks has a loyal audience and regularly attracts between one and two million viewers for each episode. This is a sizeable audience for its early evening schedule and it is one of Channel 4's best performing programmes in terms of its audience share. This makes it an attractive programme for potential sponsors. At the time of writing, it is sponsored by Nescafé, which means that there is a special *Hollyoaks*/Nescafé 'trailer' at the beginning and end of each part of the programme. These are the prime advertising slots, since they are most likely to catch those viewers who might disappear to the kitchen or the toilet as soon as there is a commercial break or when the programme has finished.

- Talk to students about their experiences of videotaping their favourite programmes. Do they fast forward through the adverts? If so, do they look out for the advertising sponsor (such as Cadbury's for *Coronation Street* or Jacob's Creek for *Friends*) to signal the beginning of the next part of the programme? What does this tell us about the effectiveness of this kind of sponsorship deal?

In addition to the Nescafé sponsorship deal, *Hollyoaks* is likely to be operating on an annual budget of less than £16 million (which was *Brookside*'s annual budget in 2001/2). This may increase slightly now *Brookside* has ended as Mersey Television may redirect the funding to upgrade *Hollyoaks*.

● Scheduling

Hollyoaks is currently screened five times a week. Its early evening screening time has varied from 6pm to 6.30pm (which is its current regular slot). The omnibus repeat has been referred to as a 'must see' programme among the 18–34 age group in the Sunday morning 'hangover zone' between 11am and 1pm.

Brookside's decline and fall has been mirrored by a general decline in Channel 4's ratings, as they have lost viewers to BBC2, Sky One and the recently re-vamped Channel 5. In this context, *Hollyoaks*' relative success in maintaining its audience share makes it an important programme for the TV channel and its scheduling is of crucial importance. The 6pm slot was originally designed to attract the target 16- to 24-year-old market, perceived by schedulers as seeking refuge from 'serious' news programming. In the past year, Channel 4 has re-organised its early evening schedule to ensure a coherent transition between audience segments. *Richard and Judy* was commissioned in an attempt to bridge the gap between the loyal but mature *Countdown* audience (mainly 55+-year-olds) and the younger 'student' audience (16- to 24-year-olds) who have traditionally been targeted by other channels in their early evening schedules.

Hollyoaks was placed at 6.30pm and was preceded by shows like *Shipwrecked* or *The Salon*. Occasionally, *Hollyoaks* is transmitted outside its early evening slot. This occurs when the controversial storylines are too explicit or hard-hitting to be covered within the ITC guidelines on what is allowed to be shown before 7pm. The male rape episodes, for example, were shown after 11pm.

- Ask students to discuss their early evening viewing habits and compare these with other members of their family. Do different age groups have different requirements and routines in the early evening?

● Marketing and press coverage

As with other soap operas, *Hollyoaks* receives extensive coverage in specialist magazines like, All about Soap and Inside Soap. *Hollyoaks*' stars are regularly featured in female 'teen' magazines like Just 17 and Bliss and in magazines like FHM aimed at the young male. There is a special *Hollyoaks* website, which gives character/story updates and general information about the programme as well as offering a special subscription service. This enables fans to participate in online chats and to receive exclusive interviews and previews.

The benefits of this kind of 'exclusive' service are mutual. Through asking members to subscribe, the TV company is able to gain detailed information about the profile of its audience, while the fans are made to feel that they are part of a wider online community, and are able to share their thoughts and interests with other like-minded people.

- Find out if anyone in the class has subscribed to a website as a fan. What do they see as the benefits of doing this? What might be the dangers or concerns which would stop people from subscribing?

● Themes

Teen troubles with a 'lite' touch

Hollyoaks is regarded as Britain's first home-based soap to specifically address the concerns of teenagers. The tone of the series is a mixture of light comedy and more demanding issue-based storylines. A recent storyline about a young couple, Chloe and Matt, arguing and breaking up, was resolved when their friends locked them in a room together and forced them to work out their problems. An added twist was that their conversation was broadcast over the college radio and listeners phoned in to give them advice. In this way, they were made to come to their senses and realise how much they really cared for one another.

This plotline was just one in a week when other storylines included a serial killer on the loose; attempts to establish a pole-dancing evening at the nightclub, The Loft; and a homeless teenager trying to maintain a 'normal' life while looking for somewhere to live. Like a traditional teenage magazine, many of the themes in *Hollyoaks* are a means of exploring the particular concerns of an adolescent audience, and in so doing, allowing the audience to consider the pros and cons of particular courses of action, without appearing to preach in an overtly moralistic manner. Nevertheless, the programme does follow moral guidelines:

> We're not missionaries, but characters can't get drunk or use drugs without consequences. (David Crean, former *Hollyoaks* producer, at a BFI conference on soaps, 2000)

The programme's willingness to address controversial issues like male rape, underage sex or problems with debt gives it a particular adult credibility in the eyes of the audience. Despite this, these issues are rarely allowed to overshadow the otherwise light-hearted tone of the show.

● The postmodern soap

Ironic pleasures
Like a teenage magazine aimed at a largely teenage audience, the programme explores adult issues and storylines while maintaining a light-hearted tone.

For older members of the *Hollyoaks* audience, many of whom watch during the 'hangover' zone on Sunday mornings, this light-hearted tone is important to the viewing enjoyment. It allows a largely undemanding or humorously engaging, sometimes ironic viewing experience while simultaneously succeeding in maintaining audience attention through the use of typical soap conventions. Watching *Hollyoaks* therefore becomes part of the weekend routine.

Ironic viewing is often seen in a 'postmodern' context, where media-literate viewers have become so familiar with the conventions of a particular genre that they can mock them, while enjoying them. Ironic viewing often implies a kind of knowledge or empowerment for the audience or a sense of being included in the 'knowing' contract between the producer and the audience (ie being intelligent or aware enough to be in on the joke).

- How ironically do students watch a soap like *Hollyoaks* or *Neighbours*?
- Do they see it as targeted for a slightly younger audience? If so, do they justify watching it ironically because of this?

Postmodern endings
Although *Hollyoaks* follows a typical soap narrative structure – half-hour episodes which have several storylines running concurrently – it employs a distinctive ending. This self-consciously draws attention to the cliff-hanger convention in an ironic and self-referential way. A short sequence after the final titles either develops the serious cliff-hanger more explicitly or is used as a quirky or humorous postscript to one of the storylines.

- Students could compare the endings of *Hollyoaks*, *Neighbours*, *EastEnders* and *Coronation Street*. In what ways are they similar or different in their use of the cliff-hanger convention?

● Locations

From kitchen sink to bathroom toilet
Unlike other British soap operas like *Coronation Street* or *EastEnders*, the title sequence of *Hollyoaks* does not draw attention to its regional location. The scrolling titles are more reminiscent of *Neighbours* and depict scenes from the programme which foreground character and past storylines. This serves to universalise the themes being explored, with the settings reinforcing this notion. The studio-based scenes within the college, near the lockers or in the classrooms could reflect the experience of students anywhere.

Nevertheless, the soap can be defined as middle class, and is set in a relatively affluent area in the north west of England. Scenes in the family homes could be said to reflect similar scenes of middle-class life in many parts of Britain. However, the scenes are not typical of other soaps, reflecting the specific target teen audience who are likely to use their bedrooms and other more individual or private rooms in preference to other group locations within the household. Scenes are therefore shot in bedrooms, toilets and bathrooms as much as in kitchens and living rooms.

- Students could compare the number of individual and group settings used in one episode of *Hollyoaks* and an episode of *Coronation Street* or *EastEnders*.
  – How does this reflect the experience of teenagers?
  – Do students recognise and identify more readily with the settings used in *Hollyoaks* than those in other soaps?

• Representations

Middle-class values are central to the programme, from entrepreneurs Tony Hutchinson and Helen and Gordon Cunningham (Mr C), who represent the concerns of running a business, through to the over-protective and moralistic parenting of Les Hunter (he throws Ellie out after finding out about her involvement in the pole-dancing night) or Will Davies (concerned about Abby's safety while trying to track down a serial killer on the loose). Regional accents are not particularly strong and neither are they markedly class-bound: suggesting a kind of ubiquitous, 'non-descriptiveness', which allows for and facilitates much wider audience identification.

The cast is largely under 30 years old. Many of the young actors have pin-up potential, and this is exploited through tie-in TV or teen magazines: a recent issue of All about Soap included posters of Helen Noble (Abby Davies) and pictures of Max Brown (Kristian) and Sarah Baxendale (Ellie Hunter). Older characters conform to traditional roles and are 'authority' figures: parents, teachers, employers and the pub landlord.

The cast is overwhelmingly white, with only one black character, Norman, in the show at present. He is currently homeless. Although the absence of black or other ethnic minority groups could be said to be representative of the Chester suburb which *Hollyoaks* is supposed to depict, the lack of any non-white faces in the programme is striking. Norman's character is positively portrayed but it is difficult to see how far he can be seen to be representative of the whole non-white community in the north west of England. There is only one disabled character: the wheelchair-bound Adam.

Family and community

Like other soaps, *Hollyoaks* is strongly family-based with a range of family groups interacting within a relatively small community; currently, several characters from the Cunningham, Davies, Dean and Hunter families are featured in *Hollyoaks*, in addition to other single characters. While a few of the families represented in *Hollyoaks* fall into the traditional category of nuclear families, issues of single parenting, divorce and re-marriage are also prominent. Overwhelmingly, the family is represented as a site of struggle, particularly since the focus is on the lives of the young characters who are often in conflict with parents and other authority figures. This might be seen to directly reflect the concerns of the target audience. At the same time, the lack of the older, stronger woman in a central controlling role (despite the regular appearance of Helen Cunningham) makes this soap very different from the other three discussed in these case studies.

Issues of sex and sexuality are covered in a frank way, with affairs (Tony and Mrs C) and underage sex (Dan and Debbie) recently portrayed. Relationships are important in *Hollyoaks* with several couples in the programme at any one time and characters' lives centring around romantic pursuit. OB even went online recently to find an appropriate cyberdate. The gender roles therefore tend to be informed by this fundamental impulse towards heterosexuality and romance and are therefore fairly conventional.

Friends – the new community

The community represented in *Hollyoaks* centres on friendship groups, around school/college, pub or business. The focus of this community is on the trials, tribulations and humour of everyday life rather than on a particular local or regional community. This is instantly apparent from the organisation of the title sequence which foregrounds character rather than place in its rolling credits.

- Ask students to analyse the title sequence of *Hollyoaks* and compare it to *Neighbours*, *Coronation Street* and *EastEnders*. What expectations does each title sequence generate about the soap it introduces?

● Ideology and *Hollyoaks*

The producers of *Hollyoaks* construct a soap explicitly aimed at young people, yet they are unlikely to be in the 16 to 24 age category themselves. Questions can therefore be raised as to how far the soap opera can represent the lives, values and opinions of the target audience accurately. Young people are not being allowed to speak for themselves in this programme.

- How strongly do students feel about this? Should a soap opera for young people be made by young people? Is this realistically possible? How might a soap producer incorporate the views, beliefs and values of young people?

Case studies

The success of *Hollyoaks* with its target audience led some commentators to defend the soap and suggest that there must be a significant degree of audience identification. However, a more sceptical critic might note that the producers of the show are in a powerful position to construct characters and narratives which can *appear* to question or challenge authority (the rebellious teenager, Ellie, for example) and yet are merely conforming to a stereotype. This 'rebellious teenager' stereotype is so commonplace, it is both instantly recognisable yet ultimately non-threatening, since any opposition is represented as a self-contained and transient phase which will be passed through and will result in eventual, inevitable, social conformity when the character matures.

Any questions posed by teenagers to the social order can be managed, marginalised and ultimately ignored. The parental concern shown towards the younger characters, or the concern of good friends towards characters who are in danger of straying off the straight and narrow, is usually privileged as legitimate. The soap therefore functions as a kind of modern day morality tale (listen to your elders, crime doesn't pay, honesty is the best policy) which functions to support society's dominant ideologies.

The fact that this is all presented in a light, humorous and entertaining package can be viewed as another ideological function itself. Is the soap successful with young audiences because it really voices their concerns or is it simply an opiate which deflects them away from real questioning or active ideological engagement with the social and political *status quo*?

- Discuss with students: Where else is the 'young rebel' stereotype found in the media? Is there an opposite stereotype: the 'conformist'? Get them to list all the current 'young rebel' storylines and characters in the mainstream soaps. What links and connections can they see? What ideological role do you think this stereotype plays in society?

Glossary

Archetype
An original template for a common character type, such as 'hero', 'villain', 'fool', 'lover' etc.

Audience
The people addressed by a programme or the receiver(s) of a message. An audience is usually grouped and defined by media commentators and producers in terms of its **demographic profile** (age, sex, race, social class, geographical location etc). **Target audience**: the specific audience a media producer attempts to reach. **Mass/mainstream audience**: a large or majority audience which dominates viewing. The opposite is a **minority** or **niche audience** which is a small group with specialised viewing tastes and habits. **Audience fragmentation**: the identification and division of the audience into particular groups by media producers in order to enable more effective targeting.

BARB (Broadcasters' Audience Research Board)
The organisation responsible for collecting audience ratings for television.

BSC (Broadcasting Standards Commission)
The organisation responsible for investigating complaints about taste and decency on television and radio.

Cliff-hanger
A narrative device which keeps the audience in suspense. It is used at the end of soap operas to encourage the audience to view the next episode.

Continuity
The need to maintain consistency in camera shots, sets or storylines to ensure they match and that 'surface realism' is continuous. For example, in **continuity editing** or **story continuity**.

Convention
An established device or set of rules used to construct a media text. These have become so widely accepted that the audience expects their inclusion.

Credits
The details of the people involved in making the programme. In soap opera these often (though not always) run at the end of the programme.

Culture
A 'whole way of life' which distinguishes a particular social group. This will include the ideas, values and beliefs shared by people within this social group. **Cultural identity** will be expressed through language and norms of behaviour which display 'belonging' to the social group. In Britain, culture can often be related to issues of class: ie, looking at **working-class culture** or the **cultural values** of the middle classes. **High culture** ('high brow') might be defined as the preserve of a powerful **cultural élite** and is usually associated with class. Thus, traditionally **high cultural forms** might be seen to be classical music, opera or ballet. In contrast, TV soap opera has often been derided as a **low cultural form** ('low brow') and has been accused of lacking any educational or intellectual value. **Popular culture** is the culture shared by the mass of the population.

Demographics
The means by which audiences are classified and mapped in terms of specific categories like age, gender, ethnicity or social class.

Form
The structure of a text which has an established set of conventions, particularly in relation to narrative. These are usually determined by genre.

Genre
The grouping of media texts into categories or types which share specific **generic codes** and **conventions** or characteristics. For example, TV soap opera is a genre which has an established set of narrative conventions. When a text contains characteristics from more than one genre it is called a **generic hybrid.**

Hegemony
The theory (taken from Italian Marxist, Antonio Gramsci) that those in power use institutions like the media to manufacture a 'common-sense' consensus, which ensures that the established power relations in society are maintained.

Hypodermic model
An audience theory, which suggests that the media 'injects' ideas and behaviour into the audience, often with negative consequences. This theory tends to depict the audience as homogeneous and as passive recipients of the messages.

Ideology
A set of views, ideas and beliefs, which are held by an individual or shared by a group. **Dominant ideology** is the system of views, ideas and beliefs, which appears to be most widely supported by influential institutions like the media. The views of those who do not support the dominant ideological consensus are likely to be **marginalised**. Because dominant ideology is so widely supported and reinforced, it quite often appears to be invisible or simply 'common-sense' (see **hegemony**).

Mise en scène
The arrangement of everything within a scene or frame, eg actors, sets, props, lighting etc.

Narrative
The way in which a story or plot is told and unfolds. **Narrative enigmas** are the questions or mysteries posed to the audience throughout the story to keep them interested. **Narrative closure** is the way in which a particular story is ended. Traditionally this happens at the end of a text, but in soap opera, because of its **multiple narrative structure**, closure of individual storylines can happen at any point in an episode (see **cliff-hanger**).

Patriarchy
The organisation of society whereby men occupy the key positions of power.

Pluralism
The idea that power is dispersed among social groups and that no one interest group is therefore able to dominate. Pluralists argue that the media represents this through the diversity of its representations.

Production
This can either refer to the product itself or the process of making the product. **Pre-production** is the preparation required before filming begins and **post-production** is the application of finishing touches after the main filming event, for example editing.

Reading
The process of decoding a media text. According to media theorists there are different types of readings available in any given text: the **preferred reading** is the way in which the text is intended to be read by the producers. This construction of the text to favour a particular preferred reading can often be unconscious, but is nevertheless one of the ways in which the **dominant-hegemonic** point of view is reinforced. **Negotiated** or **oppositional readings** occur when a viewer consciously rejects or subverts the preferred reading and constructs an alternative; for example, in male homosexual celebrations of particular female soap stars as gay icons.

Realism
The use of particular, accepted codes and conventions to construct a world which is recognisable and which audiences believe in. **Surface realism** is the conscious use of obvious, visual signifiers like contemporary dress codes or set decoration to establish a plausible representation.

Representation
The processes through which the media select, present and communicate information about the world to us.

Schadenfreude
Delight in other people's misery.

Scheduling
The placing of programmes at a particular time on a particular channel to reach a particular audience. Media producers adopt a range of **scheduling practices**, such as **hammocking** (placing a lower-rated show between two more popular ones) and **stripping** (placing the same programme or genre at the same time every day).

Stereotype
The representation of a particular group, place or issue which has become reduced to a simplified or one-dimensional perspective. A stereotype is often used to generalise (often negatively) about a subject.

Uses and gratifications
An audience theory, which investigates the diverse range of audience needs, pleasures and uses of a media text. It depicts the audience as **active** and **heterogeneous** in making choices about their media consumption.

Verisimilitude
Literally this term means 'truth-like'. It is used in soap opera to mean the appearance of being real or true or being similar to real life (see **realism**).

Bibliography and further reading

N Abercrombie and B Longhurst, 1998, *Audiences*, Sage

Robert C Allen (ed), 1995, *To Be Continued – Soap Operas around the World*, Routledge

I Ang, 1985, *Watching Dallas*: *Soap Opera and the Melodramatic Imagination*, Methuen

I Ang, 1991, *Desperately Seeking the Audience*, Routledge

H Baehr and G Dyer (eds), 1987, *Boxed In*: *Women and Television*, Pandora

G Branston and R Stafford, 2001, *The Media Student's Book – Second Edition*, Routledge

A Briggs and P Cobley, 2002, *The Media*: *An Introduction*, Pearson Education

Broadcasting Standards Commission, May 2002, *Soap Box or Soft Soap* (report)

C Brunsdon, 2000, *The Feminist, the Housewife and the Soap Opera*, Oxford University Press

D Buckingham, 1987, *Public Secrets*: *EastEnders and Its Audience*, BFI

D Buckingham (ed), 1993, *Reading Audiences*: *Young People and the Media*, Manchester University Press

D Buckingham, 1993, *Children Talking Television*, Falmer

P Buckman, 1985, *A Study in Soap Opera*, Salem House

V Clark and R Harvey (eds), 2002, *GCSE Media Studies*, Longman

V Clark, J Baker and E Lewis, 2002, *Key Concepts and Skills for Media Studies*, Arnold

M Clarke, 1987, *Teaching Popular Television*, Heinemann

A Cranny-Francis and P Palmer Gillard, 1990, 'Soap Opera as Gender Training: Teenage Girls and TV' in T Thredgold and A Cranny-Francis (eds), *Feminine, Masculine and Representation*, Allen and Unwin

G Creeber (ed), 2001, *Television Genre Book*, BFI

J Curran and M Gurevitch (eds), 1991, *Mass Media and Society*, Arnold

R Dickinson, R Harindranath and O Linne (eds), *Approaches to Audiences: A Reader*, Arnold

R Dyer (ed), 1981, *Coronation Street*, BFI

E Dyja (ed.), 2004, *The BFI Film and Television Handbook 2003*, BFI

J Ellis, 1982, *Visible Fictions*, Routledge

J Fiske, 1989, *Understanding Popular Culture*, Routledge

J Fiske, 1990, *Television Culture*, Routledge

D Gauntlett and A Hill, 1999, *TV Living*, Routledge

C Geraghty, 1991, *Women and Soap Opera: A Study of Prime-Time Soaps*, Polity

C Geraghty and D Lusted (eds), 1998, *The Television Studies Book*, Arnold

H Gray, 1997, *Watching Race: Television and the Struggle for 'Blackness'*, University of Minnesota Press

A Hart, 1991, *Understanding the Media,* Routledge

J Hill, 1986, *Sex, Class and Realism*, BFI

D Hobson, 1982, *Crossroads – The Drama of a Soap*, Methuen

D Hobson, 2003, *Soap Opera*, Polity

P Holland (ed), 1999, *The Television Handbook*, Routledge

H Jenkins, 1992, *Textual Poachers: Television Fans and Participatory Cultures*, Routledge

R Kilborn, 1992, *Television Soaps*, Batsford

T Liebes and E Katz, 1993, *The Export of Meaning: Cross-Cultural Readings of Dallas*, Polity Press

J Lull, 1990, *Inside Family Viewing*, Routledge

D McQuail, J Blumler & S Brown, 1972, 'The Television Audience: A Revised Interpretation' in *The Sociology of Mass Communication,* D McQuail (ed), Penguin

D McQueen, 1998, *Television: A Media Student's Guide*, Arnold

D Morley, 1986, *Family Television: Cultural Power and Domestic Leisure*, Comedia

T O'Sullivan, B Dutton and P Rayner, 1998, *Studying the Media – Second Edition*, Arnold

A Press, 1991, *Women Watching Television*, University of Pennsylvania Press

E Seiter, 1999, *Television and New Media Audiences*, Oxford University Press

L Stempel Mumford, 1995, *Love and Ideology in the Afternoon*, Indiana University Press

C Stewart et al 2001, *Media and Meaning – An Introduction*, BFI

J Storey, 2001, *Cultural Theory and Popular Culture: An Introduction*, Pearson Education

D Strinati, 2000, *An Introduction to Studying Popular Culture*, Routledge

P Trowler, 1996, *Investigating Mass Media*, Collins Educational

J Watson and A Hill, 1999, *Dictionary of Communication and Media Studies* (fourth edition), Arnold

Useful websites

www.bbc.co.uk/*EastEnders*
www.coronationstreet.co.uk
www.*Hollyoaks*.co.uk
www.brookside.com
www.bbc.co.uk/neighbours
www.perfectblend.net: unofficial fan website for *Neighbours*
www.merseytv.com
www.granadatv.co.uk
www.mediaguardian.co.uk
www.barb.co.uk
www.rts.org.uk: Royal Television Society

Resources

Packs on *EastEnders* and *Coronation Street* can be obtained from:
EastEnders, Room 207, Elstree Centre, Clarendon Road, Borehamwood, Herts WD6 1JF
Coronation Street, Granada Television, Quay Street, Manchester M60 9EA

Videography

As part of the merchandising surrounding all major soap operas, a range of videos is commercially available. Some are listed below. Check 'official' websites and video outlets for more recent additions.

- *Brookside* The Teenagers
- *Brookside* The Women
- *Brookside* Friday the 13th
- *Brookside* The Lost Weekend
- *Brookside* The Men
- The *Coronation Street* Years
- The *Coronation Street* Women
- *EastEnders* The Mitchells
- *Hollyoaks* Off On One, 1998
- *Hollyoaks* Indecent Behaviour, 2001
- *Neighbours* Scott and Charlene Love Story
- *Neighbours* 10th Anniversary

Acknowledgments

A very big thank you to Information and Press Offices at Elstree, Granada TV, Mersey TV and Grundy TV in Australia, especially Karen Sutherland; Nicky North and Wendy Earle at the BFI and Vivienne Clark as series editor.